Praise for
Spiritual Misfit

"This book is profoundly insightful and laugh-out-loud funny—the kind of ... ... aundry room ... ... :ading. World ... ... writer, spiritu ... ... pieces of her ... ... on the pages ... ... 1't surprised ... ... closer. *Spiritu ... ... gh the dark, ...

"Mich ... ... rspective or ... ... rough the do ... ... when you're ... ... iscover is how ... ...

... ... aazing

"It is rare to find someone who seeks God as Michelle DeRusha does—with an authenticity the world lacks, with the wit and candor of Anne Lamott, and with the humility of Christ himself. *Spiritual Misfit* is the unadulterated journey of a woman who knows what it is to struggle and what it is to overcome. You'll come away changed."

—EMILY T. WIERENGA, author of *Atlas Girl*

"Michelle DeRusha's *Spiritual Misfit* is a generous and honest portrait of stumbling into faith. This book is an invitation to wonder and journey, masterfully crafted by Michelle's insights and humor. At once vulnerable, at once assured, this narrative offers a welcome and fresh perspective on the spiritual memoir and on the coming to terms of faith within ourselves and our communities."

—PRESTON YANCEY, author of *Tables in the Wilderness:
A Memoir of God Found, Lost, and Found Again*

"This is the book we've been waiting for! It's the book we need, because there is no way we get to faith without asking a bunch of questions and fumbling around in the dark for a while. This book frees us to be ourselves with Jesus, and to let him pursue us and woo us and love us and challenge us and stretch us. Michelle tells her story with humor and heart. It's as if she knew someone needed to go first, giving the rest of us courage to exhale and say, 'Whew! I'm not the only one!'"

—DEIDRA RIGGS, managing editor, The High Calling;
founder, JumpingTandem

"Michelle DeRusha is a masterful writer who brings fresh insight, imagery, and wisdom to the spiritual memoir genre. *Spiritual Misfit* invites the reader to climb a tree and cock the head to see the world from a whole new perspective. It's funny, smart, and brimming with hope—a book for those new to faith and those who long for a faith that's new. I look forward to reading everything Michelle DeRusha writes."

—RACHEL HELD EVANS, author of *A Year of Biblical Womanhood*

Spiritual Misfit

Spiritual Misfit

A Memoir of Uneasy Faith

Michelle DeRusha

CONVERGENT
BOOKS

SPIRITUAL MISFIT
PUBLISHED BY CONVERGENT BOOKS

All Scripture quotations, unless otherwise indicated, are taken from the Holy Bible, New International Version®, NIV®. Copyright © 1973, 1978, 1984, 2011 by Biblica Inc.™ Used by permission of Zondervan. All rights reserved worldwide. www.zondervan.com. Scripture quotations marked (MSG) are taken from The Message by Eugene H. Peterson. Copyright © 1993, 1994, 1995, 1996, 2000, 2001, 2002. Used by permission of NavPress Publishing Group. All rights reserved.

Details in some anecdotes and stories have been changed to protect the identities of the persons involved.

Trade Paperback ISBN 978-1-60142-532-4
eBook ISBN 978-1-60142-533-1

Copyright © 2014 by Michelle DeRusha

Cover design by Mark D. Ford

Published in the United States by Convergent Books, an imprint of the Crown Publishing Group, a division of Random House LLC, New York, a Penguin Random House Company.

CONVERGENT BOOKS and its open book colophon are trademarks of Random House LLC.

Library of Congress Cataloging-in-Publication Data
DeRusha, Michelle.
    Spiritual misfit : a memoir of uneasy faith / Michelle DeRusha.—First Edition.
        pages cm
    Includes bibliographical references.
    ISBN 978-1-60142-532-4—ISBN 978-1-60142-533-1 (electronic) 1. DeRusha, Michelle.
2. Catholics—Biography. I. Title.
    BX4705.D29445A3 2014
    282.092—dc23
    [B]

                                                    2013043791

Printed in the United States of America
2014—First Edition

10 9 8 7 6 5 4 3 2 1

SPECIAL SALES
Most Convergent books are available at special quantity discounts when purchased in bulk by corporations, organizations, and special-interest groups. Custom imprinting or excerpting can also be done to fit special needs. For information, please e-mail SpecialMarkets@Convergent Books.com or call 1-800-603-7051.

For Brad
Because you always had faith that I would find faith

———

And in memory of Janice "Haukebo" Johnson
Your light shone
(Matthew 5:14–16)

Contents

The Beginning
of the End

Falsehood is so easy,
truth so difficult.
—GEORGE ELIOT

In third grade I stole a necklace. As I labored over fractions, nibbling a rubbery pencil eraser and spitting grainy flecks onto the floor, I spied it glinting from Kim's desk across the aisle. We all sat at those Formica elementary school desks, the ones that yawned wide open over our laps so our pencil cases and workbooks and glue sticks were readily accessible. The necklace sat right at the edge, within reach. It was exquisite, exotic—a choker with a black velvet strap and a single brilliant faux sapphire, like something Barbie would wear with a sequined halter, the red convertible top down, Ken at the wheel.

I had to have it, pined for it, battling a desire so strong it made my stomach clench. So while Mrs. Grant bent over Kim's shoulder, I quickly reached behind their backs, slid my fingers into the open desk, grabbed the velvet strand, and balled it into the front pocket of my corduroys, a snake slipping into a dark hole.

Regret rushed in almost instantly. The thrilling high of the conquest crashed into gut-wrenching fear. Aware of its weight all day in my pocket, I passed up my usual penny drops on the junglegym at recess for fear the necklace would plunk into the sand as I swung by my knees. Later I dashed to the girls' room and perched on the toilet with the gem balanced on my thigh. I thought seriously about flushing my loot but worried it would plug up the system. Plus I realized that wouldn't solve the real problem anyway, the whole rotting-in-hell dilemma. A simple flush would not hide my sin from the all-seeing eyes of God.

I never wore the necklace, of course. How could I? My mother would have noticed immediately and interrogated me; none of my relatives would have given me such a flashy piece of jewelry—we were more a mother-of-pearl crowd. I couldn't even tell my best friend, Andrea. I knew she'd rat me out to her mother, who would then tell my mother, and I'd be history.

Occasionally, with the door of my bedroom tightly closed, I held the choker up to my neck before the mirror—I never dared latch the clasp—to admire its sparkle and dream of how it would look with my rainbow-striped velour top, wishing I could wear it to Heather's roller-skating party. I realized it was pointless to own such a gem when I couldn't flaunt it, but it was too late to put it back.

Stealing, I knew, was a ticket straight to hell. "Thou shalt not steal" was, in fact, one of the more clearly defined commandments. I may not have fully grasped the nuances of "Thou shalt not covet thy neighbor's wife" or "Thou shalt not bear false witness against thy neighbor," but there wasn't much fuzziness around the seventh commandment. I could practically hear God thundering, "Thou shalt not steal...Michelle."

Breaking a commandment was a mortal sin, especially when the act was premeditated, and I knew I had definitely schemed to get that necklace into my pocket. While venial sins, like fibbing or gossiping, might land you in Purgatory for a few decades if you failed to confess before you died, the unconfessed mortal sin would send you spiraling directly to the eternal fires of hell. I knew if I didn't do something soon, I was destined to shrivel up in hell like a clam neck in the Frialator.

Thankfully, I had an out: all I had to do was confess my sin to Father Loiselle. My mother dragged my sister and me to Saint Michael's for confession once a month and every Friday during Lent. And I loved it. Well, not the act of confession itself. That was like visiting gnarled Aunt Bell in Mount Saint Margaret's nursing home and having Dr. Mallard's gaggy fluoride treatment, all at the same time. But oh, that feeling: the lightness that spread like a warm wave through my body after I exited the confessional. Nothing, nothing came close to that heady burst of liberation as I danced down the church steps, my soul pure and unblemished once again. The hope! The promise! The possibility! *This time, I swear, I'm going to be good. I am so done with sinning!*

Each month I steeled myself, buoying my spirits with a pep talk. "Okay. This is it. Yup. Here we go. You can do it. Seriously, no problem. I mean, aren't there worse sins than stealing? Like murder, you know, something bloody and gross, like the guy who stuffed his wife's body through the wood chipper. That's way worse than stealing some dumb fake necklace. Just get in there and do it."

After drawing aside the red velvet drapes, I crept into the dim confessional and knelt before the grated window, hands clasped, white-knuckled and clammy. The window whooshed open, and from the shadowy figure hunched on the other side came a quiet voice: "You may begin, my child."

Wait, wait, did he say "my child"? How the heck does he know I'm a kid? Shoot. Crap. Shootshootcrapcrapcrap, can he see me?! "Bless me, Father, for I have sinned. It's been one month since my last confession and these are my sins: I lied to my mom and dad; I disobeyed my parents; I kicked my sister on the couch while we were watching *The Love Boat;* I called Andrea a dork."

Give or take a few minor infractions, I recited the same list every time, and I always left off the big one; I simply couldn't bring myself to confess the theft. I would leave the confessional uncleansed, kneel in the pew to recite my penance, and curse myself for my cowardice. Had there been a flagellation whip at hand, I would have used it in an instant, anything to gain a feeling of atonement.

After some months of this, my soul started to feel like my mother's Sunday T-bone, smoldering on the grill about ten minutes too long and shrunken to a blackened lump.

Finally, after about the fifth failed confession, I came up with a brilliant idea: I would start wearing a scapular. A scapular is a "sacramental"—a religious object worn by Roman Catholics. It's commonly given to young children when they make their First Communion, which was exactly when I had received mine. My scapular consisted of two small squares of cloth connected by a loop of thread and worn over the shoulders, so that one square rested on the chest and the other on the back between the shoulder blades. It was of the "brown scapular" variety (nicknamed for the color of the cloth)—officially called the Scapular of Our Lady of Mount Carmel—and it was authentic, having been blessed by a priest before it was given to me.

Ordinarily I kept the scapular in a small wooden box on the bookshelf next to my bed. But when I decided to take it out, drape the threads over my head, and nestle the two squares under my clothing, I did so for one reason and one reason only. Inscribed on the scapular in gothic script was this line: *"Whosoever dies wearing this scapular shall not suffer eternal fire."* This, I felt, was like Monopoly's much-sought-after Get Out of Jail Free card. This was my loophole, my free pass into heaven. All I had to do was keep the scapular on my body, and I would be saved.

The use of the scapular is steeped in tradition and mystery. It's believed to have been originally given by the Virgin Mary to Saint Simon Stock, who, legend has it, lived in the hollow of an oak tree as a young boy before joining the Order of the Carmelites in 1212. When he appealed to Mary in a prayer for his oppressed order, it's said she appeared before him with the scapular in her hand, saying, "Take, beloved son this scapular of thy order as a badge of my confraternity and for thee and all Carmelites a special sign of grace; whoever dies in this garment, will not suffer everlasting fire. It is the sign of salvation, a safeguard in dangers, a pledge of peace and of the covenant."[1]

With the scapular tucked beneath my clothes I felt invincible, as if I were wrapped in an invisible, magical cloak, a shield of protection. So what if it was a bit of a hassle? Sometimes it wrapped itself two or three times around my neck and threatened to strangle me as I slept. And sometimes it slid into the folds of my turtleneck, rubbing a raw spot until I had to flee to the girls' room to straighten it out. The rule was that you had to wear the scapular all the time, even under your soccer uniform and your nightgown. Unsure how bathing worked, I stashed it on the sink counter and splashed through my shower at breakneck speed, hoping I wouldn't slip on the soap, crack open my head, and plummet straight to hell. For weeks I turned down open swim night at the town pool. After all, I couldn't very well display the scapular over my bathing suit like a nun.

To me, wearing the scapular was worth all the trouble. Its presence released me from fear and allowed me to feel free and safe again. The constant chafing of the rough fabric against my skin was a reminder of my sin, a penance of sorts. In my mind, the subtle but ever-present discomfort was an atonement, a substitute for the fact that I hadn't actually confessed my sin to a priest. I told myself it was okay because I was doing something better; I was making an even greater sacrifice: I was wearing a scapular every day for the rest of my life! It also helped that the scapular was hideous; it was fitting that I forced myself to wear an unattractive accessory in place of the sparkling, alluring necklace. The scapular—rough, primitive, and ugly—was exactly what I deserved.

I never connected the scapular with any thoughts about God; it never occurred to me that I should first have faith in God before I expected the scapular to make good on its claims. I simply wore it as proof, like a legal deed granting me the "right" to enter heaven. I wasn't exactly sure who was granting me this right—the priest who blessed the scapular and gave it to me on my First Communion? Jesus? God? But that didn't matter. I simply figured if I followed the rules just right—wore those two squares of cloth appropriately and didn't ever remove them from my body—then the inscribed words would come true.

At the time I hadn't known about Mary's message to Simon, but even if I had, I surely would have missed the nuances of her speech. I certainly would not have appreciated that she meant the scapular to be merely a symbol of Simon's faith and a sign of grace. It wasn't the pieces of cloth that bore any power, but the faith behind them. Mary stated her intent clearly when she emphasized to Simon that the scapular was a "*badge* of my confraternity," a "*sign* of grace," a "*sign* of salvation," and a "*pledge* of peace and of the covenant." Whether the priest made that distinction clear when he handed me the scapular, or whether I chose not to hear it, I don't recall. All I know is that I considered those two squares of cloth my passport to eternal life.

Eventually, inevitably, I lost the scapular. I'm not sure if it got tangled in my sweater and was sucked out with the dirty water in the washing machine, or if the strings wore thin and it slipped out the bottom of my shirt and onto the street. All I remember is that I discovered one evening to my absolute horror that the scapular was gone. I searched frantically for it, pawing through the hamper, retracing my steps through the apple orchard in back of our house, scanning the hallways of Mountain View Elementary the next morning, peering into the stalls of the girls' room, and combing the soccer field. But it was gone.

Once again I was defenseless, stripped of my armor, gripped by terror, and bound for the unquenchable fires of hell.

———

Thinking back, I'd say the stolen necklace and the scapular debacle were the beginning of the end of faith for me. Of course I still attended

Mass. When I was a young child and all the way through my high school years, my mother didn't allow any other option. I got a pinch squarely on my thigh if I didn't genuflect correctly, so voicing doubt would surely have been frowned upon. Yet when it came time to recite the opening line of the Nicene Creed, I always cleared my throat or yawned at exactly the right moment to avoid saying, "We believe in one God, the Father Almighty..." It was that easy. Ignoring a single line of prayer allowed me to skirt the truth.

The truth was, I didn't really believe in God. I was an impostor, a charlatan. I gargled my way through church week after week, clearing my throat during the "We believe in one God" line of the Nicene Creed so I didn't have to lie audibly. Apparently I figured uttering the line aloud would have been a blatant deception, while coughing it was less of a sham. I prayed my fake prayers, signed sympathy cards, "You're in my thoughts and prayers," followed the rules and danced the dance, not really believing in my heart yet refusing to admit my lack of faith, even to myself. I was so good at faking that I even tricked myself into a false belief, a pretend belief, because I was too afraid of the alternative. No God meant my life would end with my death.

As a child and teenager, my fear of death compelled me to maintain my facade of faith. While most girls my age were trying to figure out how to get Shaun Cassidy to fall in love with them, I had more pressing concerns. Dread crept over me at bedtime like a San Francisco fog. I lay in the dark and gnawed my fingernails, tasting iron blood on my tongue, raking my hands through my hair. Occasionally I stumbled out to the family room and complained of insomnia to my parents. Dad lay sprawled on the couch watching TV, while Mom paged through the paper in the recliner, her nubby terry-cloth robe pulled up over her ears to ward off the chill. One night they let me sit with them for a few minutes; *The Omen* was on TV. What were they thinking? That perhaps a few delicious minutes with the Antichrist would lull me peacefully into slumber? I still remember the scene in which the 666 birthmark is discovered etched into Damien's scalp. Not realizing the significance of the digits, I misinterpreted the numbers as a set of devil's horns sprouting from the boy's head, an image that made for a decidedly poor night's sleep.

My dad, a high school guidance counselor, probed with innocuous questions about the source of my insomnia: "Are you having trouble with your teachers? Are you getting along with your friends? I know you're worried about those math word problems, honey."

How could I tell him the truth? That I lay in bed holding my breath, eyes squeezed shut, limbs splayed, trying to experience what it felt like to be dead. I could not wrap my mind around it—I'd be dead…and people would still grocery shop. I'd be dead…and people would still mow the lawn, eat ice cream, brush their teeth. Everyone would go about their business, and life would go on. Except for me. I'd be dead.

My grandmother's puzzling illness fueled my anxiety. One January day she began to have trouble breathing. Within a few hours she was hunched over her kitchen table, wheezing and gasping for air. Aunt Kathy whisked her to the emergency room, where they ran a battery of tests, all of which proved inconclusive. My grandmother's condition worsened overnight, and by the next day she was no longer breathing on her own. When we visited her in the intensive care unit of Mercy Hospital as she lay in a coma, I refused to enter her dim room, and my parents didn't force me. Even though I was in high school then, I was terrified of the hospital: the strange smells—urine and meat loaf and cleanser—the glaring fluorescent lights, the PA blurting foreign codes. From the hallway I stared through the plate glass window into my grandmother's room, the half-closed blinds only partially obscuring her face. Her eyes stared wide, blankly, frozen open as her chest shuddered to the rumble of the ventilator.

She was dead within a week. Gramma's condition had continued to worsen daily despite the dramatic intervention, until my mom and her siblings decided to take her off the life-support system. I missed the wake and funeral, complaining of flu-like symptoms and difficulty breathing. I remember lying in bed, sleepless, the night of the wake, long after my parents and sister had returned home and gone to bed themselves. I was gripped with fear, my hand resting on my chest as I monitored my breathing, worried that I had "caught" Gramma's bizarre virus, convinced I would die of whatever illness had taken her life so swiftly.

I'm not sure where this paralyzing fear of death originated; after all, it wasn't as if I'd never been introduced to the concept before. Quite the opposite, in fact—I was a wake maven.

Uncle Jack's was my first. I was eight and wearing my flouncy Easter dress that fanned like a square dancer's when I twirled. Sampson Funeral Home was pretty—the carpet a plush cotton-candy pink, velveteen wing chairs nestled cozily next to gleaming tables, each with a crystal bowl of peppermints, the red-and-white-striped ones wrapped in crinkly cellophane.

Dad and I filed into place at the end of the respectably long line and reviewed the protocol. "Kneel at the coffin, say a prayer, don't touch anything, don't forget the sign of the cross," he said, rattling off instructions as if they were the Saturday chore list.

When the time came to pay our respects, I walked slowly up to the coffin with my head bowed, lowered myself onto the kneeler, and peered into the casket through slitted eyes. Crossing my ankles daintily, I smoothed the folds of my dress, made the sign of the cross, and tried to think of something to pray about. I didn't know Uncle Jack well; this was not a sentimental farewell. My bland prayer took only a few seconds, allowing me ample time to stare at the body.

At first glance Uncle Jack looked just as my mom had said he would, like he was sleeping in a suit, tucked inside the periwinkle satin, hands clasped around a rosary. But the longer I stealthily peered, the more it seemed something was a bit off. Uncle Jack's cheeks looked a little too peachy. And why did his fingernails seem so...plasticky? Come to think of it, his mouth was kind of bunched up, sort of like he was sucking on a Sour Patch Kids candy. As I knelt beside Uncle Jack, I had the overpowering urge to touch him, just the slightest graze of my fingertips against those plasticky nails. Would he feel chilly? hard? squishy? I leaned in closer. Was his chest moving? His chest was moving. He was breathing. Uncle Jack was alive! He was alive and sucking on a Sour Patch Kid!

I inhaled sharply. My dad glanced down at me, and I was just about to alert him to Uncle Jack's true condition when I felt a hand on my shoulder. "He looks good, doesn't he?" My head snapped back, bouncing squarely off Aunt Alice's bosom as she leaned in, White Diamonds and mint Polident mingling with the stench of gladiolas. I nodded in agreement, but what I really thought was, *Uncle Jack looks like a giant ventriloquist doll. A giant ventriloquist doll eating a Sour Patch Kid.*

Generally wakes and funerals in my Irish Catholic family were an excuse for a party. A death offered an opportunity to break out the booze and plug in the Crock-Pot of meatballs. The adults sipped scotch on the rocks and hit the smorg, while we cousins played kick the can in the backyard and stole blonde brownies off the dessert table. Sure we'd all been weeping a couple of hours ago, sure it felt a little weird to enjoy seconds of the baked ziti while Uncle Jack was barely in the ground, the AstroTurf tucked around the edges of the muddy hole, but I got used to the order of events: mourn and bury; drink and eat. The post-funeral festivities distracted me from the death. Enticed by the cookie platter and the Irish soda bread, I didn't have to think about who was inside that mahogany coffin—Uncle Jack with his bunchy lips and too-peachy cheeks.

I never thought to talk to my parents about my fear of death. I never thought to question them about my doubts. Questioning—in fact any conversation about religion, God, or faith—was not condoned in my family. Although my parents never explicitly forbade such discussions, somehow we kids understood that religion was off-limits. God didn't pop up in conversation at the dinner table. He was rarely even mentioned, aside from inclusion in the routine bedtime prayer. And he certainly was not woven into the fabric of our daily lives. Rather, he was relegated to church—God lived within the confines of Saint Michael's or Saint Joseph's or whatever church we were attending at the time. Instead of talking to God, or even talking about God, we went to church. I memorized a handful of prayers and recited them dutifully at Mass. I made monthly trips to confession and endured a half hour of Mass every Saturday evening, as well as on the occasional Holy Day of Obligation.

God was not accessible in an everyday kind of way. He was like a foreman or a CEO—distant and important, someone you might approach with a serious concern, but not someone with whom you made small talk. Not that God was uncaring, exactly, but rather, as the Big Boss in the sky, he was an authority figure who was not to be questioned. As a child, I never nurtured a real connection to God because that kind of relationship was never presented as an option—not in church, not by my priest, and not by my family, who were my spiritual role models. Frankly my family members' basic beliefs were as mysterious as my religion itself.

When I was young my dad occasionally went with us to church, but he never took communion. Instead he sat stiff and upright in the pew with his arms crossed. He grabbed our pant legs with a poker face and the hint of a smirk so we had to shake off his fingers as we filed by. As a kid, I often wondered why my dad didn't do communion. Was he harboring a deep, dark sin? Did he not believe in the sacrament, the body and blood of Christ? If he went to the effort of attending church, why not go all the way and take communion? My dad was curious; that much was clear from the eclectic mix of reading material, from mysteries to science to theology, piled high on his bedside table. But did he believe in God? That was the central question, and of course one I never asked.

A few years ago Buzz—that's what everyone calls my dad, including my sister and me from time to time—joined a men's Cursillo group. He began to attend monthly meetings and even went on a weekend retreat. "What? Seriously, Mom, is he having some kind of midlife crisis?" I gasped when my mother told me Dad was away for the weekend with a bunch of men on a church retreat. He seemed invested, but I was skeptical. Initially I assumed he was faking belief out of fear, much like I did, panicking as he inched closer to death and pretending to find God. I just could not believe my dad had found religion, and even more, that he had found God.

As time went on, I became persuaded his newfound spirituality was genuine. I sensed a shift in Buzz. Some of this change was manifested in outward appearances: he attended church regularly; he also took communion and still participated in his monthly Cursillo group; he even received a daily e-newsletter from a Benedictine monk at a nearby monastery. But the transformation seemed to resonate even beyond that. My dad became quieter, less likely to bark orders, criticize, or snap angrily. He was more contemplative, peaceful even. He seemed present, more in the moment rather than distant and distracted. There was an ease about him that I had never seen before.

More recently my father cared for a dying friend. My dad had known Jimmy and his wife, Mim, for decades. They were all part of the same "group," a gang of couples that formed during their college days and stayed intact through marriages, child rearing, careers, and deaths. I wouldn't say Jimmy and my dad were extremely close through the years; they weren't best friends in the typical sense. But they traveled in the same circles. Maybe that's why it was even more surprising when my dad stepped up in Jimmy's last weeks as he slowly succumbed to colon cancer. For a month or so Buzz spent four or five nights a week in their home, sitting in the dim bedroom through the night, holding a moistened sponge to Jimmy's lips, combing his hair, offering him morphine, engaging in a bit of conversation if Jimmy was restless or anxious.

Hearing about this experience—mostly through what my mom told me, since Buzz didn't elaborate on the details—I was awed and inspired by my father's courage and selflessness. And I began to believe that it was my dad's strengthened connection with God that had allowed him to participate in Jimmy's dying hours this way.

While my understanding of my dad's thoughts and ideas about faith was ambiguous at best, my mom was a much easier nut to crack. My mom has always had what you would call blind faith. She trusts that God will take care of her, life be what it may. Honestly, I've sometimes been a little bit envious of my mom's no-questions-asked confidence. I've wished I could pull into the fast-faith drive-through and order up. "Ah, hi, yes, I'd like number 3...the Blind Faith, please... with a side order of patience." So easy, so painless: no decisions, no angst, no waffling, no questions.

Once I asked my mom out of the blue, "What would you do if Dad died?"

Her answer was simple: "I'd be okay. I have faith that I'd be okay." I believed her. She's never been a "Hallelujah!" "Praise Jesus!" soapboxy, in-your-face kind of believer. Just the opposite; my mom— whom we often call Mo, for Maureen—has always been as matter-of-fact about her faith as she is about most everything in life. Mo is practical, even-keeled. She isn't overly emotional or expressive, and she doesn't embellish. She once described childbirth as feeling "like bad menstrual cramps." (A remarkable understatement, as I later discovered for myself.) Growing up, I could measure my mother's religious commitment simply by how resolutely and faithfully she attended Mass and visited the confessional. Her steadfast determination and loyalty, week after week, year after year—regardless of whether or not her husband attended Mass—over time resulted in a quiet but firm proclamation of faith, mounting evidence of her belief.

At some point I realized my mother didn't attend Mass out of a sense of obligation, but out of genuine desire—or at least a combination of both. Yes, she had to be there every weekend and on Holy Days of Obligation, but she wanted to be there. I never asked my mother why, or how, she believed in God, because I always knew what her answer would be: a matter-of-fact "I just do." She would not, or perhaps could not, elaborate or explain. She wouldn't dissect or defend. She simply believed.

This blend of religious ambiguity and uncertainty in my childhood years did not give me a clear picture of what religion, and more important, faith, really was. We didn't read the Bible together—we didn't even have a Bible visible in our house. We didn't talk about heaven and what kind of "place" it might be (although hell was mentioned with some frequency). At best I got cryptic references to heaven, and more often, no mention at all. In my family, religion wasn't something you talked about. Religion was something you simply did. This, my parents told me much later, was how they were raised as well.

My weekly catechism classes, as I remember them, added little to my sketchy understanding of faith. There, I recall, I memorized the Ten Commandments and heard a lot about Satan and hell; a little about an amorphous, disconnected God; and hardly anything at all about Jesus. The images of hell I "got"; those pictures made sense to me. A roiling inferno teeming with screaming, writhing sinners was a much more tangible picture than pearly gates, billowing clouds, and wispy figures in flowing white robes. An eternity in hell was much easier to envision than an eternity in heaven.

Confession only confused me further. The brief high of absolution and atonement was followed almost immediately by the inevitable tumble back to the brink of hell, with the cycle repeating itself over and over again for months and years. And once I stole that necklace, of course, all hope was lost. The threat of eternal damnation dangled over my head, tainting my days with fear and anxiety. It never once occurred to me to confess my sin directly to God and ask him for forgiveness. As I understood it, that was not an option.

While some of my childhood role models—my mother, for example—demonstrated faith in their own ways, I couldn't see a clear picture of how faith operated in real life, or at least a picture that made sense to me. I needed something more than the proclamation, heartfelt though it was, that everything would "be okay." I needed something more tangible, something I could dissect and question, something with which I could wrestle…and not feel like I was sinning in doing so. The God of my childhood, as I understood him, was reachable via the limited channels of confession and Mass, and that just wasn't enough for me.

In retrospect, it's no surprise that I began to rely more and more on what I could guide, determine, and control with ease. Myself.

2

My Excel
Spreadsheet Life

> Deep in the human unconscious is a
> pervasive need for a logical universe
> that makes sense. But the real universe
> is always one step beyond logic.
>
> —FRANK HERBERT

I attended church a couple of times with my Catholic girlfriends as a freshman at the University of Massachusetts, not to find God but to find a boyfriend. The message conveyed by the priest may have differed from the one I thought I knew, but I never listened long enough to find out. Instead I scanned the young men as the communion line filed past my pew, appraising their combed hair, button-down oxford shirts, and wrinkled khakis. After a few halfhearted visits to the campus chapel, I gave up on Mass altogether. Aside from the requisite attendance with my parents on Christmas and Easter, I didn't cross a church threshold for four years until, a few months into graduate school, I met Brad.

Brad hails from Minnesota, the birthplace of stoicism, the place where people ice fish for fun. Minnesotans drive a pickup out to the middle of a frozen lake, saw a chunk out of two feet of ice, drop in a line, and plunk down on a milk crate in a negative-forty-degree windchill that frosts eyelids, freezes the deepest recesses of the nasal passages, and frostbites exposed fingers in 13.5 seconds. Ever been to Minneapolis in mid-January? It's fourteen degrees, and people are out exercising in short sleeves, practically picnicking on the shores of Lake Minnetonka.

Minnesotans are tough, and I'm not referring solely to their tolerance of weather akin to Dante's ninth circle of hell. They don't complain, they don't grimace, they don't bemoan their bad luck. "Oh sure, yah, just goin' through a bit of a rough patch here, doin' just fiiine." Both Brad's mom and grandmother endured cancer and all its indignities with exactly that attitude, as if they were weathering a bad stretch of hangnailitis.

Brad finds comfort in statistics, research, and facts. Maybe it's because he comes from a family of lawyers, but wherever he gets it, his levelheaded attitude melds well with his Minnesota stoicism. Every time I freak out he spouts stats like a Yellowstone geyser, citing evidence, for instance, as to why our Boeing 747 will not, in all probability, plummet from the sky. Meanwhile I'm convinced I'll perish in a flaming crash each time I set foot on an airplane. After all, it *does* occasionally happen to someone. Some poor soul boards the plane, Starbucks and *Glamour* in hand, settles into her seat, adjusts the air vent, and then careens to her death en route to Las Vegas or Orlando or Paris. It happens. So what's to say it won't happen to me?

Suffice to say, Brad is one of the most rational people I know—a quality that, in my mind, didn't seem to mesh well with a belief in God. When I first learned he was a practicing Lutheran, I was puzzled. *How could someone so grounded, so logical, have such a deep faith? How could someone who approaches everything with such reason believe in something that seems so illogical?* I wondered. Not only was Brad an active member of the Lutheran church, he also seemed to be an authentic believer. While he wasn't overtly religious—he didn't proselytize and he wouldn't ever ask you if you knew Jesus Christ—he was quietly but passionately faithful. I couldn't figure him out.

When we first met at the University of Connecticut, Brad belonged to Ebenezer Lutheran, a simple clapboard church that loomed over the potholed streets of Willimantic. I began to attend services with him a few months after we started to date. After all, rolling out of bed together on Sunday morning didn't seem like the best time to launch the "I'm not really a believer" conversation. Plus I was eager to impress. Here was a great guy with great hair. He was smart, funny, and kind. So he believed in God and I sort of…didn't. Well, I figured we'd just deal with that detail later.

Brad's minister at Ebenezer, Pastor Cheryl, seemed "normal," and by that I mean she was not like any ministerial types from my childhood. Warm, effusive, and huggy, with a soaring voice and a big laugh, she was married, had a kid, and wore Bermuda shorts to the annual picnic. Pastor Cheryl knew every parishioner by name, even mine by the second week. She was like a female Santa Claus, her eyes crinkling in amusement, her face open and welcoming. And Ebenezer itself was surprisingly pleasant too. Not exactly coffee-and-a-Krispy-Kreme-in-bed-on-a-Sunday-morning pleasant, but still, the people were friendly and we belted out rousing hymns like "Go Tell It on the Mountain" and "A Mighty Fortress Is Our God." I left feeling energized and cheerful; so what if I tuned out during the prayers and sermon?

I introduced Brad to the depths of my disbelief drip by drip, over a period of years. There were early indicators, such as my not-so-subtle refusal to discuss God and all things related to religion or spirituality. I think it's amusing and ironic that I married a man with a master's degree in Divinity Studies. Could I have picked a more inappropriate candidate for my lifelong mate? Inappropriate because of course he loved to discuss religion and theology—Brad delved into all things theological like I deconstructed Carrie Bradshaw's outfit on last night's *Sex and the City* rerun—and of course, at the time we met and even after we married, I was desperate to steer the conversation to less murky waters.

After numerous failed attempts to engage me in theological discussion, Brad finally let it rest, not buying the "I don't do deep thoughts" excuse, but not quite sure where I stood on God either. When I finally got around to telling him that my faith was tenuous at best and nonexistent on most days, he suggested there might someday come a time when I would face circumstances that would compel me to turn to God. In 1997 opportunity knocked.

———

Two years into our relationship, while Brad was still a doctoral student at the University of Connecticut and I was working as an assistant editor at a magazine in New York City, I came down with a sudden and mysterious illness. It began with a stomach bug on Valentine's Day, but instead of improving after twenty-four hours, new symptoms bloomed one after the other: swollen glands, throbbing headaches, pressing fatigue, skin rashes, a nagging cough. Several weeks into the illness my hair began to fall out, drifting to the floor as I dried it, strands tangling into wispy balls and blowing around the bathroom like tumbleweed. When I finished blow-drying, my arms limp from the exertion, I crouched on my hands and knees with a dustpan and broom, swept up a pile of hair, and dumped it into the wastebasket.

I was so constantly nauseated I could choke down only a single blueberry at a time. As a result, I dropped fifteen pounds in a matter of weeks; even my underwear was too big, pouching around my hips and sagging like a stretched-out swimsuit. A few months prior I had run my first marathon; now I could barely stagger the six blocks from Grand Central Station to my office. I struggled to concentrate at work, eyes blurring, muscles twitching. My thoughts scattered like milkweed fluff; words wouldn't come when I needed them. I wondered if I'd had a small stroke.

Over my lunch hour I stumbled to Barnes & Noble to page through chapters on diseases of the digestive and immune systems in the *Mayo Clinic Family Health Book* (this was pre-Google, after all). I then presented my symptoms to one doctor after another, beginning with my general practitioner and running through an exhaustive list of referrals: gastroenterologist, neurologist, rheumatologist, infectious disease specialist, psychiatrist. I offered pints of blood and eagerly endured invasive tests and procedures, hoping for a diagnosis and relief from the horrifying thought that I was dying. Blood work, x-rays, endoscopy, sigmoidoscopy, colonoscopy—all revealed nothing.

I worked myself into a frenzy as I searched desperately for a disease that matched my symptoms, convincing myself of one dire possibility after another and getting tested for each: HIV, multiple sclerosis, lymphoma, Crohn's disease. I was frantic that a test would come back positive and frantic when it didn't. I even got tested for HIV twice, the second time sneaking off to a free clinic downtown, too sheepish to admit to Brad that I was convinced they had accidentally switched my initial test results with a healthy person's. Paralyzed by fear, I lay awake at night tortured by thoughts of what it would be like to die a long, slow, agonizing death. During the day I gazed out my living room window and watched the garbage collector dump my trash, wishing desperately that I was he, so lucky to have the energy to lift a trash barrel, so lucky to be going to work.

After multiple office visits and dozens of negative lab results, my primary care doctor was clearly done with me. "Nothing's turned up; the tests are all negative," Dr. Feinstine told me coldly as I sat on the examining room table, the soft blue gown tucked around my thighs, goose bumps running down my calves. "It's a virus. You'll just have to wait it out." A moment passed between us. Too tired to argue, I stared at him, and he stared back, shifting from one foot to the other with my file under his arm, one hand on the doorknob. "Call the office if you need to come in," he advised in a clipped voice.

Sleep, ironically, was one of my biggest problems. You would think a person chronically exhausted, a person left trembling and breathless after a twenty-five-foot walk down the driveway to the mailbox, would collapse into a dreamless slumber each night. Strangely that was not the case. It wasn't just my roiling, twitching muscles or the constant pain that kept me awake, but a deeper, more startling sensation. Though I was tired, my body hummed with a strange electricity, as if it were a hive, buzzing with the activity of ten million worker bees deep inside. More than simply the inability to relax, it was a tension, as if I were a high-voltage electrical wire crackling with a dangerous current.

One night, frustrated and despairing, I popped an Imipramine on top of the two Tylenol PMs—which were about as effective as Alka-Seltzer for my insomnia—that I'd swallowed earlier. Dr. Feinstine had prescribed the antidepressant in a last-ditch effort to shut me up, but I hadn't tried it yet—I wasn't *that* crazy, was I? The tiny pill slid down my throat with a gulp of water, and I returned to bed.

Fifteen minutes later I wasn't at all sleepy, but strangely, it seemed my nose had morphed to three times its size. I touched it gingerly. It felt the same as usual, but I was too afraid to look in the mirror, half expecting I would resemble one of those creepy, bulbous-nosed monkeys from Borneo. Weirder still were my hands. They looked normal, resting atop the sheet, but they felt humungous and fuzzy. My fingers felt like balloons. In fact my entire hand felt as though it had been twisted into a balloon animal, an octopus or a cobra or a poodle on a leash. I was mesmerized—not sleepy, of course—but mesmerized. When I reported the incident the next morning to my parents (I'd taken a leave of absence from my job in Manhattan and gone home to Massachusetts to try to recover), they were stunned silent. Later I found the Imipramine bottle stashed behind a framed photo on my dad's bedroom dresser. I think they thought I was trying to kill myself, but really I had just wanted a decent night's sleep.

"She's depressed," my father concluded, hauling me off to a shrink the afternoon after the Imipramine incident. This was Buzz's way of corralling his worry: take action, "make it happen," as he always advised my sister and me when we were mired in indecision.

Truthfully, I had never seen him so anxious. I think he had started to believe my claims that I was dying, that I most definitely had contracted something ravaging and incurable. I remember him sitting on the edge of the twin bed as I lay there one stifling August afternoon, my neck sweaty, my hair fanned out over the pillow in a tangled mess. "What can I do, Shelly?" he asked, his eyes tearing. "I don't even know what to do." My dad, always in command, always in control, was at a loss.

Thankfully the psychiatrist saw that I was indeed depressed—depressed because I had been sick for two months with a mysterious, undiagnosed illness. He confirmed a point I had been belaboring for weeks: I was not depressed in a clinical sense but was sick and therefore depressed as a result of my illness. Finally someone understood that I felt as if I'd been run over by a road grader, that I was defeated by the fact that my morning deodorant application was often my singular accomplishment for the day. Finally someone understood that while *that* fact was indeed depressing, I was not depressed, at least not clinically depressed. There was a difference.

At last I got what I was searching for: a diagnosis. It wasn't anything terminal, as I'd assumed. Nor was it lupus, Lyme disease, multiple sclerosis, or any of the other serious diseases I'd investigated. As it turned out, I was finally diagnosed with an illness I had vaguely heard of before, but one that I'd brushed off with disdain: chronic fatigue syndrome.

"What? There's no way it's that; please, please, run some more tests," I begged Dr. Rosati, the physician I'd been seeing since I returned to Massachusetts. I knew about chronic fatigue syndrome, and I did not—I repeat, I did *not*—have that. Chronic fatigue syndrome was for middle-aged housewives, hypochondriacs, people with "issues." I, on the other hand, had something serious, something terminal or at the very least tropical, not some crazy lady, rich girl pseudovirus. Certainly not the "Yuppie Flu."

Alas it was indeed the "Yuppie Flu."

Back in the 1980s when the name of the syndrome was first coined, and even into the mid-90s, chronic fatigue syndrome (CFS) was considered by many to be a wastebasket diagnosis, handed to a patient when absolutely all other possibilities had been eliminated— when the doctor was at a complete loss but the patient was still pressing for an answer. Few doctors took it seriously; most wrote it off as textbook depression, or worse, hypochondria, malingering. Dr. Rosati was remarkably compassionate, and he seemed to view CFS as a legitimate illness, but frankly I was embarrassed by the diagnosis. Part of me wished I had something dire, something that sounded as horrible as I felt, something I could explain in important-sounding medical jargon to my friends and coworkers. But no. I felt like a flighty, fainting nineteenth-century woman with a case of the vapors. I was ashamed.

And I was in a quandary. I didn't have the energy to butter a slice of toast, never mind schlep back and forth to my job in the city, work fifty hours a week, and function as a normal human being. My employer had graciously allowed me to take several weeks of paid sick leave as I jaunted from doctor to doctor. But once I had the definitive diagnosis, I knew I couldn't stay in New York. So I quit my job at the magazine and officially moved back in with my parents. My life consisted of sleeping in a twin bed surrounded by my high school track trophies, watching *Sanford and Son* reruns, and eating Hamburger Helper at the kitchen table. There I was: twenty-five years old, sick with a bizarre illness, jobless, and living with Mom and Dad. Now *that* was depressing.

Nobody got it, of course. "So you're, like...*tired*?" friends would ask incredulously. How could I explain without sounding like a total flake? That "tired" meant I couldn't even walk to the mailbox at the end of my parents' driveway without resting on the curb before making the return trip to the house. My arms were so weak, just pulling a T-shirt over my head left me dizzy and breathless. I couldn't read, I couldn't go out, I couldn't talk on the phone. For hours at a time I would sit in a rocking chair on my parents' porch, the wooden floorboards creaking softly beneath the runners, or lie on the salmon-colored carpet in the family room while my dad vacuumed around my prone body. When friends called to check on me I motioned to my mom, who held the phone in her hand, to tell them I was sleeping. I didn't have anything to talk about, aside from my latest muscle twitches or the results of my most recent blood work or the *Barney Miller* rerun I had watched at 1 a.m. the night before—not exactly fodder for riveting conversation. This is the problem with a chronic illness; after a while it gets to be old news, and there's not much left anyone can say.

I learned as much as I could about CFS. I was shocked to discover—even though the name pretty much spells it out—that CFS is, in fact, a *chronic* illness. Many of the people I met in the local support group had battled the illness for nine, twelve, fifteen years—not working, fighting years-long disability cases, on good days achieving a shower and a change of clothes or a walk around the block. I had assumed I would eventually recover fully, but now I faced the terrifying possibility that I would end up like one of them: sick, lifeless, and dependent on my parents forever.

So this, you're thinking, was the moment, right? The moment Brad had predicted. The moment I looked heavenward and put my life in God's hands, the moment I relinquished control and gave myself over to Jesus. In retrospect, it would have been a good time for a religious conversion. In reality, asking God for help never even crossed my mind. Instead I did what I always did: I took the matter into my own hands. *I* would control my outcome; *I* would make myself better; *I* would get over it; *I* was not going to be a loser.

I started to exercise, first walking down the driveway and back, then increasing the distance bit by bit: to the end of the street, around the block, one mile, then two. I radically altered my diet: became a vegetarian, bought the whole series of Moosewood cookbooks, slashed sugar, caffeine, alcohol. I got as much sleep as I could, swallowed handfuls of vitamins, and explored meditation, t'ai chi, and homeopathic medicine. I also networked. I dialed up complete strangers—friends of friends of friends whom I had heard suffered from CFS—and pumped them for information. That was how I found an infectious disease doctor in New York City who specialized in CFS. I dragged myself back and forth to Manhattan for appointments and learned how to administer injections of Kutapressin—a broad-spectrum antiviral derived from pig livers—daily into my thigh.

Then I quit the CFS support group. After I had gleaned all the information I could, I stopped going to the meetings, severed friendships with group members, and cut myself off from the nonrecovered. I was determined not to be one of them—dependent, weak, and useless.

Throughout all of it, Brad stayed the course. My mom nagged about COBRAing my health insurance plan, my dad insinuated that it was "the Fitzgerald Syndrome" (Nana and her siblings, with their persnickety bowels and tension headaches, were considered chronic hypochondriacs), and my friends inquired whether I was "better yet." But Brad believed in two things: one, that I had a real illness; and two, that I would recover. On my darkest days as I lay in bed and wept, he would repeatedly reassure me, "You will get better. You will recover." I didn't truly believe the words, yet I yearned to hear him speak them again and again. *You will get better; you will recover. You will get better, you will recover.* As if hearing them uttered aloud would somehow make them true.

Brad didn't bring up faith or God or the value of suffering, but I knew it was his faith that kept him steady and gave him the courage to encourage me. While I drafted complicated lifestyle plans, still consumed on the inside with dread and fear, Brad supported me in every way. He empathized, sympathized, cheered, and comforted, all the while exuding a reassuring confidence that I would recover.

That's the beauty of faith. When all else fails, when you lose control and hit the bottom, when everything you thought was true vanishes, when everything you depended on evaporates, you still have God. I didn't, and at the time I didn't care—I was still under the impression that I was in control of my life.

I eventually recovered from CFS, although my immune system has never been the same. I still succumb to every cold virus that wafts within sixty feet of me. I read somewhere that there are more than two hundred distinct varieties of the common cold, and I figure I've endured just over one hundred so far. This is good news; I'm halfway to the point of becoming immune to acute viral rhinopharyngitis.

About a year after the diagnosis I went back to work part-time as an office assistant. I filed, answered the phone, and typed memos. It wasn't exactly magazine editing, and Enfield, Connecticut, was a far cry from Fifth Avenue, but simply being able to say I had a job made me feel real and legitimate. A year later I applied for a position at a local community college.

"What am I going to say if they ask about the giant gap on my résumé, the whole year that I didn't have a job?" I asked Brad before the interview. "Can I make something up? Can I say I was traveling in Bangladesh?" Turns out the committee did ask, and I told the truth. Well, not the entire truth. I didn't admit I suffered from the disreputable-sounding chronic fatigue syndrome; I referred to it vaguely as an "autoimmune disease." The college hired me as a public relations assistant, and I was soon back to business as usual (albeit at a slightly less frenetic pace). And with my life back on track, I focused on the next step in my master life plan: marriage.

———

Unfortunately for me, we were required to enroll in a few weeks of spiritual counseling if we wanted to be married by Brad's minister. Given my reluctance to talk about God, the meetings were awkward for all of us. Pastor Cheryl pressed and I hedged, because the truth was, I *still* could not admit out loud that I didn't believe in God. I preferred to beat around the bush, convincing myself and everyone else that I was simply "not very religious." The alternative was still too terrifying. An admission of no God meant no life after death. An admission of no God meant someday I would be the one with the plastic-looking fingernails while the living, breathing people grocery shopped and plucked their eyebrows. To fake my belief was better than facing the terrifying truth of no life after death. Besides, standing alone to proclaim atheism was far too intimidating. Ninety-eight percent of the world's population believes in a God, in some form of religion. Was I unique enough, bold enough, rebellious enough to stand alone in the 2 percent? Absolutely not.

The truth is, I was never rebellious enough to claim true atheism. The closest I've ever come to rebellious behavior was during my under-graduate years at the University of Massachusetts, when I dated an anarchist and lived rebellion vicariously.

At first the whole anarchy thing was appealing. Chris was mysteri-ous. He toted dog-eared copies of Emma Goldman and William Godwin in his backpack and smoked hand-rolled cigarettes at a Northampton coffee shop called the Haymarket Café. He attended secretive meetings, managed the radical underground newspaper on campus, and drank whiskey instead of Busch. We would sit for hours tucked into a castoff couch propped on the sloping front porch of my rental house in Amherst, talking late into the night. I loved the spirited conversation, but I thought the whole anarchy thing was a bunch of ridiculous bunk.

"So, you're telling me you think the country, the world, would run more efficiently without the constraints of government?" I'd ask in-credulously. "Don't you think humanity would spiral into chaos? Don't you think maybe as a species we require the guidance and struc-ture of government?" Chris would patiently explain his philosophy and views as I lobbed skeptical questions at him. I couldn't wrap my mind around an existence without structure and hierarchy.

Of course we all know how this particular story ends. Settling down with an anarchist as my lifelong mate was about as likely as me marrying Donny Osmond. I figured the anarchy thing was a phase; that Chris would snap out of it as we inched toward graduation; that he would get a job at Hartford Life, buy a Honda, start saving for a mortgage.

Instead, around April of our senior year as I was busy trying to secure a graduate teaching assistantship at the University of Connecticut, Chris announced his own aspirations: after commencement he would move to New York City to live as a squatter.

"A squatter? What the heck is a squatter?" I asked, suspicion creeping into my voice. I had never heard the term before, and when I learned what it was, I panicked. "How am I going to visit you in New York if you're living in some run-down crackhouse abandoned apartment building, freezing your butt off in a sleeping bag, and eating Doritos for lunch with a bunch of deodorantless weirdos?" I yelled. "Will there be a shower? With hot water? Will you have your own room? Will I be able to plug in my curling iron?" As I fired questions at him, Chris just looked at me with a mixed expression of pity and disdain. "Why can't you be normal?" I fumed. "Why can't you go to graduate school or write a novel? That's revolutionary enough—why don't you write a novel about being a squatter?"

My point is this: I was, and still am, a highly rational, analytical, and structured person (with the exception of my irrational fear of flying). I'm concrete. I like chicken breast baked in a real oven; a toilet that flushes; electrical sockets that pulse with energy; my down comforter on an actual mattress, on an actual box spring, on an actual bedframe. I don't squat, and I will never squat—unless you're referring to the exercise I resurrect occasionally when my thigh jiggle gets out of hand. I was not and am not a rebel. I march to the beat of a regular old drummer.

I organize my spice rack alphabetically. I bring trash bags brimming with outdated clothes and the occasional shirt that looks really, really bad on my husband to the local Goodwill every month. My grocery list is laid out in Excel according to Super Saver's aisles. Vacuuming brings me the glow of pure joy, washing dishes is therapeutic, and my idea of the perfect afternoon would be organizing my junk drawer—if I had one.

In short, I have always liked a precisely ordered universe. I crave order and structure, love the rational, and have an unflagging zest for control. And so it makes perfect sense that I had difficulty fathoming God, someone I couldn't see, hear, feel, smell, or touch. Someone I couldn't control or mold to meet my own needs and expectations. Someone I couldn't define. Naturally I also had great difficulty imagining heaven, a place I couldn't see. A place no one—except those white-light-near-death-experience crazies—had returned from in person to describe.

God and his unfathomable mysteries did not fit into my everything-has-a-place-and-an-order-and-an-explanation world. What I didn't quite realize at the time, of course, is that you can't lay out life in an Excel spreadsheet. I may have preferred a precisely ordered universe, I may have craved structure and control, but that's not what I was going to get.

3

Lost on the Great Plains

Every step in the dark turns
out in the end to have
been on course after all.
—John Tarrant

Four years into our marriage Brad and I relocated from Massachusetts to Nebraska to launch the next phase of our lives. He had landed a job as an English professor at a small liberal arts college near Lincoln. I had resigned from my job as a writer at a financial services company in Massachusetts and would arrive in Nebraska fat, cranky, and nearly nine months pregnant with our first child.

When I'd first heard the news that we would be moving to Nebraska, I tried to be a good sport, really I did. For a full fifteen minutes I embraced the adventure. After all, there was something to be said for the take-to-the-open-road excitement, the tiny bit of smugness I felt. *At least I'm moving beyond my hometown…at least I'm adventurous…at least I don't live two doors down from my parents,* I thought to myself.

After I had exhausted my window of positivity, though, I found myself reeling from the realization that I was moving to number three on my short list of the top three worst places to live in the continental United States. Nevada, North Dakota, and Nebraska, in that order.

I had only a dim expectation of what I would find in Nebraska, stereotypes really: the easygoing midwesterner, corn-fed, robust, salt of the earth. To be frank, few New Englanders have any clue what the Midwest is like, nor do they care.

The nurse who taught our Lamaze class back in Massachusetts even suggested the medical community in Nebraska might not use epidurals in childbirth, noting casually, "Well, I'm not really sure exactly what they do for pain medication out there." I noticed she waved her hand a little in the air when she said the words "out there," as if she thought Nebraska were located perhaps near Pluto.

I thought she was joking. She was not.

"Seriously? You're telling me I'm moving to a state where the epidural may not be standard childbirth protocol! What do they use, Novocain?" I asked sarcastically. She couldn't say for sure.

Truthfully, I wasn't much more informed than the Lamaze instructor. I had crafted a jigsaw puzzle of the Midwest gleaned mostly from Hollywood and the media: Tom Brokaw's one-minute mention of drought on the plains; a photograph of a combine slicing through a sea of grain; an aproned Meryl Streep in *The Bridges of Madison County*. I'd seen the movie *Fargo*—my father-in-law was even born near Fargo. Half of Brad's extended family talks just like Police Chief Gunderson. But I knew so little about the real Midwest I could hardly fashion a picture in my mind, couldn't construct an expectation. I couldn't even pinpoint Nebraska on the Weather Channel map as the forecaster skimmed through a cursory look at the nation's midsection. Scrambling to orient myself amid all those rectangular blocks stacked neatly atop one another from Oklahoma to North Dakota, one looking just like the next, I panicked. *How can I live in a state I can't even find on a map?*

Before I left Massachusetts my colleagues threw me a corn-themed going-away party. After all, the only thing New Englanders know for sure about the Midwest is that corn grows there. We all sat around the office enjoying the corn smorg—corn dogs, corn on the cob, popcorn, cornbread, corn chowder, and cornflakes. Then my coworkers presented me with a mock cover of the corporate magazine I'd helped produce each month, my husband and me as the models, our heads planted awkwardly onto the bodies of the famous *American Gothic* couple.

You know the painting: the stoic, unsmiling farmer and farm wife, lined faces speaking years of drought, pests, and plummeting grain prices. The man grips a pitchfork, eyes piercing through wire-rimmed spectacles; the woman stares vacantly to the side, buttoned into a prim pilgrim collar cinched with a brooch and draped with a calico apron, her hair parted down the middle and pulled into a severe bun. There we were, Brad and I, in costume, playing the part of downtrodden midwesterners, our faces smiling. I laughed out loud when I saw it. "Oh, you guys are good…so clever, witty captions, too cute…"

But I wasn't laughing inside. It wouldn't be long before I was living my plain-Jane, boring, wholesome Nebraska life, a faded calico apron tied around my waist and a thin-lipped grimace on my face. *American Gothic,* I thought bitterly. *That's me.*

———

As it turned out, my colleagues had been right about the corn. Oceans of it stretched from the front bumper to the horizon. I gazed out the U-Haul window, the landscape transforming from the lush, rolling hills and crumbling rock walls of New England to the belching smoke-stacks of Gary, Indiana, and finally to the corn as we made our way from Massachusetts to the Great Plains. While the land was as broad and open as anything I had ever seen, cumulus clouds hovered low, pressing down, seeming to skim the roof of the truck as we sped across the highway. I felt oppressed by the sky and declared to Brad that clearly the clouds were a lot lower in the Midwest, although he assured me it was merely an optical illusion.

When we finally pulled off the exit ramp on the outskirts of Lincoln, I spotted a gigantic concrete building near the side of the road. It was eerily lit by rows of fluorescent lights and spanned at least several blocks along the highway. "What is *that*?" I gasped. Like the massive peeling hull of a battle-scarred warship at dock, a grain elevator loomed over the street. The thing hadn't seen a fresh coat of paint since the Nixon era, and it was humongous, diminishing the railroad cars bumping beneath it to diminutive Thomas the Tank Engine trains. It was so shockingly ugly, so Dust Bowl depressing, I half expected to see a Dorothea Lange mother and her hollowed-eyed kids propped up against it. Staring out the windows of our U-Haul as we pulled into the Super 8 lot on my very first night in Lincoln, I cried. And for my entire first year in Nebraska I avoided that part of town whenever I chauffeured my East Coast friends and family on the requisite "Heartland Tour." I didn't want them—those acquainted with cedar-shingled homes on the shore, gleaming glass skyscrapers, and quaint clapboard churches nestled snugly into valleys—to see that hulking monstrosity.

The day we moved into our house I was sent to the grocery store on a food run. Nearly nine months pregnant, I couldn't help Brad and my parents and in-laws haul bulky boxes and furniture into the house, so I was tasked with getting lunch.

As my grinders and Coke slid down the conveyor belt, the cashier turned to me with a question: "Likethatinasack?"

"I'm sorry...excuse me?" I answered, smiling.

"Likethatinasack?" she asked again, all garbled and running together with a hint of twang.

"Oh, um, I'm sorry. What did you say?" I asked again, now reluctant to meet the cashier's eye.

"Do...you...want...that...in...a....*sack*?" She articulated each word slowly, loudly, holding up a plastic bag and pointing at it with a magenta fingernail. Gray permed heads turned, the shoppers eager for a little ruckus on a languid summer day.

"Ohhhhhh...*a bag.* Yeah, yeah. Please. A bag would be great." I nodded my head and smiled broadly, hoping to convey that I was not, in fact, a total moron.

Could she tell? I wondered. Was it now clear to everyone standing impatiently in the checkout line that I didn't belong? The realization was sharp, sudden: it should have been an ordinary, everyday transaction. But it wasn't. I had landed in a foreign country. I was an outsider. I didn't even speak the language.

Move-in day was deceptively breezy and crisp. But the very next after-noon, a ferocious wind barreled up from Texas, bringing all of Houston's heat to Lincoln. It seared my eyes dry as I stepped onto the driveway, the concrete blasting heat like a furnace. It was hot. Really hot. I shrank from the blinding light like a vampire and complained unceasingly to my husband through the following days: "Why is it so windy?" "Could my hair look any messier?" "Could I be any sweatier?" "When is this heat wave going to break?" "I sweat just stepping into my underwear, for crying out loud."

Every night I tuned into the local news, fixating on the forecaster as he casually displayed the seven-day outlook: seven round glowing sun icons, seven daily highs of 98 degrees. And then the realization hit: The weatherman never used the phrase "heat wave." Because it wasn't, in fact, a heat wave at all. It was simply summer in Nebraska.

There had been hints along the way.

"Every house has central air!" I had marveled on the phone to my mother from the motel when we came to Lincoln house hunting in March.

"Really?" she'd gushed, and I had read in her tone, in that single word, her immediate conclusion: *Nebraskans have money! Who knew?* The summer we moved in, of course, we learned the truth. Most Nebraska homes have central air because you can't live without it. Come June, pull down the storm windows, draw the blinds, crank down that thermostat, and whatever you do, don't touch the car door handle with your bare hand.

With the searing temperatures of summer also came the grasshoppers. I'm not talking Jiminy Cricket here—delicate, kelly-green, chirping, daintily hopping grasshoppers. I'm talking army-green and gargantuan, hurtling from a hosta like some kind of *Mission Impossible* agent of the insect world, bouncing off your bare legs with a *thwap*. These were grasshoppers who made eye contact. And if they happened to land on you, they clutched their prickly, spiny legs with the strength of a barnacle and regurgitated a foul brown fluid that looked like to-bacco juice down the length of your limb. I was not in love with the Great Plains grasshopper.

And then, just when I thought I'd seen the worst of Nebraska, with its Depression-era grain elevators, blistering heat, and combative grasshoppers, I discovered something even more baffling. I'd been plunked into the middle of Cornhusker country.

The Cornhuskers—more fondly known as the Huskers—are the University of Nebraska–Lincoln's five-time-national-champion foot-ball team. But the Husker phenomenon goes far beyond that simple descriptor. Come game day, as I learned that first autumn, the city of Lincoln blazes red. Week-old infants tuck plump legs into red Husker Onesies, Husker caps perch on the balding heads of elderly men, and everyone—*everyone*—wears red. I, of course, forgot to wear red nearly every Saturday during that first football season, but it never took long for me to realize my fashion error. The moment I stepped foot outside my house almost every person I saw was outfitted in Husker red. And it's not only the clothing that bears the Husker "N." Homeowners display granite slabs emblazoned with the Husker logo on their front lawns; a mailbox two streets over is molded into the shape of a Husker football helmet. My neighbor flies his Husker flag at half-staff on the days the team loses, and the neighborhood collectively mourns. I swear there are even more red cars in Nebraska, per capita, than in any other state.

I also noticed that not only was the game broadcast over loud-speakers throughout the grocery store, it was even piped out to the parking lot, because clearly it would be a crying shame if fans missed a critical play between parking the car and scurrying into the store. And for whom was this effort made? Save three elderly ladies and me, the store was always deserted. The mad rush for Budweiser and Ruffles had taken place hours before.

I actually attended a live Husker football game at Memorial Stadium in Lincoln a few years after we moved to Nebraska. It was another sold-out game in a streak that hasn't been broken since 1962. More than eighty-five thousand fans crammed into the stadium hours before the kickoff, row upon row bathed in scarlet. Even the hot dogs were red—Fairbury franks, made in Nebraska. As I stood in line outside the stadium to buy a red visor adorned with the Nebraska "N," I mentioned to Brad that it was my first official piece of Husker gear. The woman in front of me wheeled around. "Are you from out of state?" she gasped, her face contorted into a phantasmagorical mix of horror and disbelief, like she was witnessing horns sprout from my scalp instead of a girl buying her first Husker visor for the bargain price of $24.99.

I offered what I thought was a perfectly rational explanation: "Oh, I'm not originally from here. We moved to Lincoln a few years ago." This was clearly not the right thing to say. The woman visibly struggled to process why in heaven's name it had taken me *years* to purchase my first Husker accessory.

While the Husker mania was troubling, it still wasn't the most unsettling aspect of my new environment. Not by a long shot. No, the thing about Nebraska that made me feel as if I would never, ever fit in and would always be an outsider was the fact that I was surrounded by avid churchgoers. I, the person so totally uncomfortable with God-talk that I could not even engage my own husband in a conversation about religion, the woman so befuddled by her own beliefs that she coughed her way through Mass, was suddenly tossed headlong into the Bible Belt like a perch flopping wildly in the bottom of a rowboat. Before moving to the Midwest, I had assumed that the nation's Bible bangers settled snugly in the South, say, any state below the Mason-Dixon line. I hadn't realized America's Bible Belt marched straight through Lincoln, Nebraska.

Time and time again I was startled by Nebraskans' comfort with discussion of all things religious. Take, for instance, this question, posed with frightening regularity: "So, what church do you belong to?" Or worse, this inquiry: "Have you found a church family yet?" A *church family*? Come again? I didn't have a blessed idea what a church family was, so I certainly hadn't been looking for one.

Asking an acquaintance in Massachusetts what church she belonged to—or, heaven forbid, if she had a "church family"—would be like asking her pants size. You did not go there. In New England, religion was a private, personal affair, a taboo topic and decidedly politically incorrect; God was not discussed over coffee and blueberry muffins. But in Nebraska it seemed God was fully present, always around, dancing lightly in and out of conversation and ambling into the room for a bite of muffin himself. References to religion, church, God, Jesus, and the Bible permeated everyday life.

One day my neighbor, a sweet stay-at-home mom, asked outright if she could pray for my family and me. Lonely and worried, I had just confided to her that Brad was in Minnesota visiting his brother, who had recently been diagnosed with esophageal cancer. Her reaction, though genuine and compassionate, took me completely off-guard and left me stuttering for an appropriate response. Never in my life had anyone asked outright if he or she could pray for me. And never in polite small talk, as casually as if we'd been discussing the best place in town to buy watermelon. This woman and I barely knew each other; we'd exchanged just a handful of greetings in the year since we had first met, and now she wanted to pray for my family? Startled, I felt like she had crossed an invisible line, exposing the private, personal sphere right out in public.

This same neighbor, I later discovered after I had kids, tagged all the Halloween candies she handed out to trick-or-treaters with the homemade label "Jesus Is the Real Treat." "What is this all about?" I said to Brad as I held up a tagged Milky Way. He shrugged. I grimaced and rolled my eyes. Apparently we lived two doors down from Martha Stewart on Jesus.

Suffice to say, Nebraskans assumed I was religious. They assumed I attended and belonged to a church, that I didn't cough through the Nicene Creed, and, a no-brainer, that I believed in God. During my first several years in Lincoln, I found myself often dodging deep questions, and it didn't take long for me to realize that admitting skepticism would not be a surefire route to forming friendships. I felt compelled to hide my real, doubting, irreligious self. After all, I wanted to make friends. I wanted to find my place. So I did what I thought I had to do to fit in: I kept pretending I believed in God.

As the months passed I worked diligently to make Nebraska my place, to find comfort, security, and a sense of belonging in an unfamiliar environment. I studied the landscape as if I were enrolled in a Nebraska topography course. On several occasions I even drove my car out to the country and parked in a dirt ditch to take photographs of the landscape, hoping the images would help familiarize me with a foreign land.

But it didn't take long for me to realize that, despite my best efforts to carve a new home for myself in Nebraska, my sense of place was gone. My foundation, the ground itself, had been swiped from beneath my feet. I had never realized how my place—New England, Massachusetts, my home ground—had defined me, until one snowy afternoon, just a few months after our move to Lincoln, I snuggled under my grandma's afghan on the couch and picked up Edward Abbey's *Desert Solitaire* off the coffee table.

The opening paragraph stunned me:

> Every man, every woman, carries in heart and mind the image
> of the ideal place, the right place, the one true home, known or
> unknown, actual or visionary. A houseboat in Kashmir, a view
> down Atlantic Avenue in Brooklyn, a gray gothic farmhouse
> two stories high…a cabin on the shore of a blue lake in spruce
> and fir country…there's no limit to the human capacity for the
> homing sentiment.[1]

I laid the book down and stared out the window at snow swirling against the empty sky. Where was *my* ideal place, my right place, my one true home? Was it really Massachusetts? I wasn't so sure. The landscape was comfortable in its familiarity, and of course my entire extended family was there, but did I yearn for it? Did my soul stick to it? Massachusetts was certainly comfier than Nebraska, with its oppressive sky and dirt-brown landscape, but was cozy like a well-worn sweater enough to qualify it as my one true home?

I know definitively that I had a "right place" at one point, when I was a kid. Sun Valley had been my true home. While Sun Valley may sound like a Pollyanna commune, it was actually a campground nestled beside a lake in the rolling hills of central Connecticut. We lived there all summer in a trailer parked at a campsite complete with a picnic table and fire pit.

Going to bed in the camper was the best part of the day. Better than hunting for elusive lady's-slippers bobbing next to stinky skunk cabbage, the woods cool and buggy, the forest floor spongy with pine needles beneath my sneakers. Better than bellowing, "Put another nickel in, in the nickelodeon..." into the crooked twig of a microphone as we hunted for glinting mica in the brook's sandy bottom. Better than crunching raw spaghetti straight from the box, anticipating the sweet Ragú and buttered Italian bread, steam rising from the Dixie plates my mom plunked onto the picnic table. Even better than sitting by the popping campfire as dusk settled, my marshmallow flaming like a kerosene lantern on the end of the sharpened stick. Going to bed was even better than all that.

My sister, Jeanine, and I snuggled into sleeping bags laid over our bunk mattresses. A filmy shower curtain hanging from a rod separated our bunks from my parents' sleeping quarters, where the dinette converted into a double bed. Jeanine's sleeping bag was much newer than mine, a slick, chocolaty nylon that swished when she moved, the soft cotton interior patterned with green-and-gold mallards and cattails. I envied the bag from the moment my mom bought it at Caldor on sale; it even smelled new compared to my ugly, musty old thing. I slept in my dad's army castoff, an olive-green, military-issued bag, branded "Property of US Army" on the exterior, its plaid wool insides rough on my bare legs.

We both knew I had the better bunk, though—the one perched over our campsite like a castle turret. The tiny rectangular window in the upper corner slid open, and from it I could glimpse the hunched backs of my parents and their friends, their aluminum chairs scraping the pea gravel as they inched closer to the flames. Sometimes they made popcorn. The buttery smell of Jiffy Pop bursting from the tinfoil pan and mingling with the sweet, woody scent of the campfire made my mouth water as I lay in my bunk. I would listen for the clink of the metal Coleman cooler, the rustle of hands in ice cubes, and the sharp pop of the Busch tab as their voices rose and fell, a murmur punctuated by sudden laughter, then a murmur again.

"Now what are they doing?" Jeanine would whisper from an arm's length away. And I'd narrate the night, play by play, until we got sleepy, the whippoorwill calling from the birch tree.

Sun Valley was, in Edward Abbey's words, my right place, my one true home. There I had been truly comfortable and in my element. But that was three decades earlier. I had lost that right place long ago. Now even the familiar comforts of Massachusetts had vanished, replaced by apocalyptic weather, grasshoppers the size of Cornish hens, and grown men wearing foam Husker corncob hats.

In a lot of ways, moving to Nebraska felt like moving to a foreign country. Surrounded by Jesus-is-the-real-treat neighbors and crushed by the vast sky and endless landscape, I felt unmoored, displaced, as if I had just arrived from Lithuania or Macedonia or somewhere much farther away than Massachusetts. I didn't fit in. I couldn't find my place or my people. My move to Nebraska wasn't merely a relocation. It was a *dis*location. I was stripped bare of my comforts, routines, safety nets, and support networks. Most of what I had known and loved my whole life had vanished and, along with it, my sense of self.

I'd never before considered how my identity was tied to my place. Happily tucked into my New England hometown, surrounded by oaks and maples, lakes and streams, crumbling stone walls and curving, dipping roads, I'd never realized how my place defined me until I was no longer there. On top of that, I had no friends, no family within fifteen hundred miles, no job, and no sense of self. In their place were a distracted husband with a brand-new job, a long-distance phone bill that rivaled Madonna's bra budget, and a grumpy infant who would not for the life of me stop crying.

Noah was born one month and eight days after we arrived in Nebraska. I could not have been more unprepared for my new role as mother. Seriously. I'm not talking we-didn't-quite-get-the-nursery-painted unprepared. I'm talking what-have-I-done-to-my-life unprepared. I had never baby-sat, not once, not even for fifteen minutes, in my entire life. I had never changed a single diaper. I had always declined to hold newborns, leery of their flopping heads and fragile limbs. I hadn't the slightest idea what to do with a baby.

Brad and I had uncomfortably giggled our way through Lamaze

class back in Massachusetts in the weeks before we moved. While other couples oohed and cooed over the birth videos we watched in class, we looked at each other in horror, both clearly thinking, *We are so screwed*.

The whole process was utterly unreal, right from the first. Sitting on the toilet with the e.p.t. stick in my hand, I yelled from the bathroom to Brad, who was holding the directions in the hallway, "What's two blue lines mean again?" When I opened the bathroom door, my first words were, "How are we going to pay for college?" When I was newly pregnant, I couldn't imagine getting fat. When I was fat, I couldn't imagine laboring. Before Noah was born I practiced getting used to the idea of a baby by peering into his empty crib, leaning over and stroking the stuffed lamb, trying to visualize an actual, real live baby in there. It didn't work. It was like petting a stuffed lamb in a crib. When I was in labor, I thought, *How am I ever going to push?* And finally, when Noah was born, I couldn't even imagine what living with a human baby would be like. I sat in the hospital bed holding my swaddled infant and thinking, *Now what?*

The answer: a sleep-deprived stupor and an endless flow of tears.

Noah cried nonstop from the second he exited the womb until he was about four months old. Before he was born, Brad and I had believed those inane parenting books, the ones that glibly noted the infant would be so exhausted from worming his way through the birth canal he'd sleep like a hibernating bear for the first twenty-four hours.

Our precious firstborn screeched like a rabid hyena for forty-eight hours straight.

Brad paced around the hospital room sweating while I tried to get the hyena to latch on to a nipple that was cracked open like a glacial crevasse. I was also simultaneously squeezing the ice pack between my legs to staunch the bleeding from my stitches. The intern who had witnessed the birth came by the next day to check on me. "Wow. How ya feelin' today? That sure was the worst tear *I've* ever seen," he said, genuinely awed. Note to interns: this is *not* what you say to a new mother who has just birthed a rabid hyena.

Brad and I were too paralyzed with fear and exhaustion, while trying to live up to the expectation of what kind of parents we were supposed to be, to insist that the nurses cart Noah away to the nursery for a couple blessed hours of respite. Oh no, we had read all about the benefits of "rooming in" in *What to Expect When You're Expecting*— the absolute necessity of "bonding" with your newborn.

The situation only worsened at home as I struggled to learn how to breastfeed and pump properly. When Noah wasn't attached to one of my breasts, I was hooked up to the Pump In Style electric breast pump. Exactly what was stylish about it, aside from the fact that the mechanical parts were all neatly housed in a leather briefcase, I wasn't sure. I sat on the living room couch holding two funnels suctioned to my breasts—which, by the way, had ballooned two cup sizes in five days. The tubing attached to the top of the funnels snaked over to the rumbling machine, while the bottom portion of the funnels fit snugly over the plastic bottles. Frankly the whole ensemble vaguely resembled some kind of medieval torture device…and it felt like one too. I absolutely could not tear my eyes away from my nipples, which had grown to elephantine proportions as they were mechanically pulled to and thrust from the suctioned funnels. Yeah, baby, I was pumpin' in style.

Just when I thought I couldn't possibly feel more humiliated, Brad walked through the room. Or I should say Brad rolled into the room.

He was mimicking a robot, jerking his limbs and head in rhythmic harmony timed perfectly to the mechanical wheezing of the pump. The imitation was spot-on, and it made me laugh, until I realized with profound certainty that I had sealed the deal. *That's just great,* I thought, still holding the funnels in place. *He's never, ever, ever going to have sex with me again.* Not that I wanted to have sex ever, ever again, but still.

Noah would not stop crying—and his was not a cute kitten's mew but a full-blown howl, as if someone were plucking out his toenails one by one. We balanced his car seat on top of the washer in spin cycle to try to vibrate him to sleep. We walked mile upon mile with him sniveling in the stroller. We snapped his car seat into our Saturn and drove him around every street in Lincoln in the dark of night. We danced soothingly with him in the living room, singing lullaby after lullaby. We tried the swing, the bouncy chair, the jogging stroller, the mobile.

And he cried.

And I cried.

I finally strapped him into the BabyBjörn and wore him on my chest all day like a snuffling tumor. I wore him while I cooked, while I vacuumed, while I dusted, and even while I went to the bathroom (this last one took some finagling, but it was doable). And when Brad walked in the door from work, I detached Noah from my chest and handed him over still wrapped in the cocoon-like Björn. Brad would strip off his sport coat and tie, then strap on the baby, while I fled to the bathtub to cry some more.

At Noah's four-month checkup I burst into tears in the pediatrician's office. I felt like a failure, I told the doctor. What kind of mother couldn't get her baby to stop crying, ever? What kind of mother didn't enjoy being a mother, ever? I told him I wasn't cut out for mother-hood, that I'd clearly made a mistake. After Dr. Donahue reassuringly cited research indicating that a mother's anxiety often contributed to colic on the baby's part (not sure whether that was supposed to make me feel better or worse), he suggested we try Noah on Nutramigen, a specialized formula engineered to alleviate symptoms of colic. At more than twenty-six dollars a can, I was skeptical. Twenty-four hours later, I was ready to purchase stock.

Noah's disposition finally improved, but mine didn't. I had as-sumed I would bounce back once my baby began cooing and smiling and acting more like a human than a hyena. I had assumed I'd start whipping up pans of brownies and humming my way through domes-tic duties with the Björn strapped to my chest. In retrospect, I probably had a raging case of postpartum depression, but I didn't know it or admit it at the time. Instead I rattled around the house while Noah napped, dusting the dustless mantel, emptying the dishwasher, and reorganizing the Tupperware drawer. I stood at the sliding glass door and gazed into the backyard, at the gray lapping gray of a Nebraska February. My family lived halfway across the country, the acquain-tances I'd met talked about God all familiar and chummy like he was the Parent Teacher Organization president, and my career had been replaced by a Merry Maids to-do list. I wound the crib mobile, folded burp cloths, and wiped smears of Gerber prunes off the dining room wall.

I was lonely and afraid, struggling to find my place and figure out my new role as a Nebraska hausfrau. Was this it? Was this my life? Was this what I was supposed to be? I hadn't the foggiest idea who I was, what my role should be, how I should define myself, or where I was going in life.

As Dante so succinctly put it, "In the middle of the journey of our life I came to myself in a dark wood where the straight way was lost."[2]

Yes, I was lost. In the dark wood of the Great Plains.

4

In Search
of Church

A path and a little
light to see by.
—ANNE LAMOTT

More than three years after my move to Nebraska I finally admitted it to myself: I had hit rock bottom. For the first time in my life I was lost and I knew it. While I made every possible attempt to restore my self-confidence and self-reliance, nothing came close to working. Believe me, I tried. I got a part-time job, took up yoga, trained for a half marathon, enrolled in a cooking class, painted my bathroom, dyed my hair, rearranged the furniture in my living room, and rearranged it back again. I even went and had another baby. But nothing pulled me out of the downward spiral. I couldn't fill the restless emptiness. I couldn't shake the sinking feeling that the person I'd been before—self-assured, secure, and in control—was not only gone, but unrecoverable.

And so, I did what a lot of desperate people do when they smack rock bottom: I went to church.

We'd actually been attending church sporadically since Noah was about six months old. We'd even church shopped for a few weeks or so. At one point we visited a small Lutheran church on the south side of town—so small that when the service was finished and we had stepped into the parking lot, I turned to Brad and said, "We are never, ever going back there." The members had been friendly and welcoming, greeting us at the door and making pleasant conversation with us on the way out. But the truth was, I couldn't attend a church where I would be recognized each week. I couldn't attend a church where people would expect me to get involved. I needed a big church, a place where I could blend in unnoticed, certainly not a place where everyone would figure out what a fraud I was. That was the main reason we chose the church we did: it was large enough for me to get lost in the crowd.

You're probably wondering why in the world I was darkening a church doorway at all, considering my lack of belief. Good question. The truth was, I was mostly trying to blend into my surroundings. Clearly Nebraskans were churchgoers. Clearly religion was a big part of life in the Cornhusker state. I was still trying to fit in, still trying to belong. Plus, Brad wanted to find a church to attend, and he wanted the kids to go to church. And honestly, I wanted that for our kids too. One would think that, as an unbeliever, I wouldn't have cared whether or not my children were exposed to religion. Yet when I looked at Brad, I saw someone much different than myself. I saw a person not floundering and lost, not restless and empty, but content and secure. I wanted to offer my children at least a chance at having what my husband's faith seemed to give him, and the best way I knew to accomplish that was to get them into a church. While church hadn't worked out so well for me as a kid, I still held out hope that it would plant the seed of true faith in them and offer, as Anne Lamott says, "a path and a little light to see by."[1]

I also wanted to protect my kids from the insidious fear of death that had haunted me throughout my childhood—a fear that, if I'd been honest with myself at the time (which I wasn't), still haunted me as an adult. I figured that if they could find faith in something greater beyond this life, they wouldn't fear death as I did.

I was the parent who refused to use the word "die" during Noah's first three years, opting instead for the euphemism "past its prime." As in, "Oh, honey, that grasshopper"—*the one baked in the sun to the consistency of a Pringle with an army of ants hauling it away limb by limb*—"that grasshopper is just a bit past its prime." During his toddler years, Noah would observe, nod, and move on, clearly not processing my ridiculous explanation. As he got older, though, he was no longer satisfied with my vague euphemisms and my refusal to talk about death. In fact, the day I stopped using the phrase "past its prime" was the day Noah asked pointedly, "Mommy, are *you* past *your* prime?"

I didn't want to talk about death with my kids because I didn't have any answers to the questions I knew would follow, such as "Where do we go when we die?" and "Do you believe in heaven?" Unfortunately, kids are curious about everything, including mortality, so they continued to press the issue, and I recall one incident in particular that forced me to talk about death with them in a very real and personal way.

Throughout the winter we had observed a large cocoon dangling like a leather satchel from the river birch tree in the backyard. We weren't confident it contained a hibernating creature—Rowan, an active toddler, had prodded it too vigorously a couple of times, batting it like a miniature tetherball, so we didn't have high hopes for its metamorphosis. Nevertheless, one May evening Noah stormed into the house shouting, "The cecropia moth is here! The cecropia moth is here!" and we all dashed out to take a look.

The moth's body was furry and plump, like a tiny fruit bat, with a wingspan as wide as my hand. Two bushy antennae sprung from its head, and on its intricately patterned wings shone two yellow spots like owl eyes. It dangled a few inches from its cocoon, gingerly folding and unfolding its giant wings, hairy legs twitching a little as they clung to the branch. The gargantuan, fuzzy moth gave me the major creeps, but the boys were mesmerized, standing so close beneath it that their noses nearly touched the moth's feathery wings as it hung upside down from the twig. They galloped up the sidewalk to summon our neighbors, John and Karna, and we all posed for photos with the moth as if it were Julia Roberts suspended from the tree. The six of us stood around the river birch for twenty minutes admiring the creature before it was time for the boys to head in reluctantly for a bath.

The next morning when the kids ran outside to inspect the moth, they discovered it was gone. We assumed its wings had warmed in the morning sun and it had flown away, but later that afternoon we learned the moth had met a different fate. Noah, who'd been roaming the yard, suddenly screamed out, covering his face with one hand and pointing at the woodchips with the other. There on the ground lay what was left of the moth, its bat body torn in two. Just a bit of the head remained, the shell of it actually, its innards presumably extracted by the probing beak of a hungry bird. Two wings lay scattered in ragged pieces on the woodchips.

Noah crumpled to the ground sobbing, rocking back and forth on his knees as I hugged him. He cried for twenty minutes straight, pausing only to inquire why I wasn't crying too. Rowan offered his brother sympathy, wandering over to give Noah a hug before running after the soccer ball, singsonging, "A bird ate it! A bird ate it! But not the wings! But not the wings!"

As his crying eased into a few sliding tears, Noah's questions began: "How did the moth feel when he died? Is the moth in heaven now? Do moths have a separate heaven from people? Will I see him when I go to heaven someday? Will I recognize him there? What if there are other moths that look just like him and I can't tell which one is my moth?"

I tried to work through his questions and offer comfort. But it was hard. Not only was my heart breaking for his loss, I also didn't really know what to say. I was afraid I would instill in Noah the same paralyzing fear of death I'd had as a child. As I sat on the warm grass with Noah's head against my chest, I realized that inside I was asking many of the same plaintive questions about death and the afterlife. And I didn't have any answers. As I fumbled through weak explanations to my son, I felt like I was constructing a plaster-of-paris theology, throwing together a glumpy hodgepodge of rambling thoughts as I went along.

Where is Brad, the man with the divinity degree, when I need him? I fumed to myself. *Why does The Waffler always get these questions?*

Finally I resorted to the truth. "Honey, I just don't know," I admitted. I told Noah that there was so much about God and heaven and how it all worked that we didn't or couldn't know. I told him that sometimes we had to try to be satisfied with not knowing all the answers, satisfied with the knowledge that someday, if we had the opportunity to hang out with God face to face, we would understand. The explanation was vague, and I certainly wasn't sure I believed it myself, but it was the best I could offer Noah at the time. I wasn't about to admit to my young son that I wasn't even sure I believed in God. I didn't want to plant the seed of unbelief in his head too.

We decided not to bury the moth. While I advocated vigorously for a dignified funeral beneath the columbine flowers—mostly because I couldn't bear the thought of my son hunched over the moth wings for the rest of the day—Noah refused. Instead he carefully lifted a wing out of the woodchips, gently blew off the dust, and carried it in a cupped palm to his room. Later I found it pinned to his bulletin board with a thumbtack, the yellow owl eye glaring eerily from the corkboard. I also spied a slip of paper on Noah's bedside table. On it, in his scraggly first-grade penmanship, was written, "Mof I love you."

So along with trying to blend in with the Nebraska natives, I returned to church looking for answers, initially not so much for myself but for my kids. Noah was beginning to ask questions that made me nervous and uncomfortable, unanswerable (for me) questions about death, God, heaven, and other troublesome topics. Passing off question after question to my theology-degree-qualified husband seemed weak, yet I didn't have much more to offer Noah than "I don't know." So I went to church looking for help. At the very least, I hoped the Sunday school teachers would fill in some of the gaps.

Brad and I took turns carting Noah to Sunday school each week.

(Rowan had a decidedly unchurchy disposition, so we alternated staying home with him.) Sometimes on my designated week I would drop Noah off in his classroom and dash over to Barnes & Noble to sip a mocha latte and page through *People* for forty-five minutes until it was time to pick him up again. But many Sundays I actually stayed for the church service. I was relieved that the "experts" in Sunday school were teaching my kid about God and heaven, but I think part of me really hoped that I'd get religion through osmosis. Like maybe if I rubbed shoulders with Mrs. Lavender Pantsuit sitting next to me, faith would stick to me like her Chanel No. 5.

At the very least it was an hour of quiet. An hour devoid of Elmo's grating giggle, Noah's relentless chatter about Mount Mountain, his imaginary place where his imaginary friend, Cricket, and Cricket's pet pterodactyl lived, and Rowan's incessant Thomas the Train whistle. An hour in which I didn't have to change a diaper loaded with acorns and stones and sidewalk chalk—Rowan used his diaper as a fanny pack, jamming in items that struck his fancy as he toddled about his day—or extract a Kraft Macaroni & Cheese noodle from a nose with a pair of eyebrow tweezers. It was, in short, peace.

I half-tuned in to the sermons every other week, and when I wasn't busy coveting the snappy wedge sandals across the aisle or defuzzing my tights, a realization began to dawn on me. Someone was missing from these sermons—someone whom I had grown to know with a disturbing level of intimacy through my previous years in the pew. The devil himself was glaringly absent from this church. He simply wasn't there, was never mentioned. Come to think of it, neither was there much mention of hell and eternal damnation. It seemed those cornerstones of my childhood religion had all but vanished in

Lutheranism, replaced by lots of talk about love, grace, forgiveness, and Jesus, and the occasional reference to sin.

You might think this would have been a relief, but ironically the absence of guilt and condemnation initially made me feel worse, more lost, more godless. It seemed like everyone else was part of some Love and Grace Club and I didn't know the secret handshake. I felt awkward and out of place, conspicuous, as if everyone could tell I didn't fit. Without hell as my spiritual compass, I struggled to orient myself in this unfamiliar landscape. Once again, I didn't speak the language.

The awkward discomfort of being the outsider reminded me of the first time I participated in a Lutheran church service with Brad's extended family. I attended my first Haukebo Reunion the year Brad and I were married. The reunion is an annual event held in Brainerd, Minnesota, for my mother-in-law Janice's extended family. Janice was one of six children, so the gathering is large, the aunts, uncles, cousins, nieces, and nephews all converging on Brainerd from a half dozen or so midwestern states. Settled among dozens of lakes and ponds, Brainerd is a smallish Minnesota town, a summer destination for campers and fishermen. A lot of Minnesotans from the Twin Cities keep summer cabins there, but Brad's Uncle Jim and Aunt Carolyn live in Brainerd year-round in a ranch-style home set on a hill above the lake.

In addition to catching a glimpse of Brainerd's claim to fame, the twenty-six-foot sculpture of Paul Bunyan that looms over Main Street, I can always count on a few other happenings during the three-day weekend. One, the kids will play endless games of baseball and kickball beneath the whispering white pines, their faces streaked like warriors, patches of dirt and grime sticking to smears of sap on their foreheads and cheeks. Two, I will gain a minimum of five pounds in three days, largely due to the tantalizing selection of hotdishes—hamburger onion hotdish, barbeque beef hotdish, tater tot hotdish—all laid out in gargantuan disposable tin vats in the garage. Three, Janice's brother, Uncle Duane, will fall asleep in a lawn chair beneath the rented tent, hands clasped across his belly, chin slumped to his chest. He usually drops off about three o'clock on Saturday, just as the sun reaches full intensity. One year the cousins propped empty beer cans around Uncle Duane's chair, crumpled in the dirt at his feet and strewn across his chest. They even slipped one into his fist without waking him and then snapped a dozen photos while he snored.

And finally, there is the Sunday morning church service. That first year, when I overheard one of the Haukebos announce that church started at ten o'clock, I assumed we would all pile into our minivans and head to the Lutheran church in town. Imagine my horror when I saw Brad's aunts, uncles, and cousins arranging the mismatched lawn and folding chairs under the striped tent, then pulling out Aunt Carolyn's Bible and placing it on the sun-weathered picnic table.

Church? Right here in the backyard? I thought. *You have got to be kidding me.*

We sat on lawn chairs, beneath the tent, on a patch of matted grass just a few steps from the garage. There were no pews, no stained glass or steeple or vestments. No altar—unless you consider the picnic table near the front of the tent. No organ or choir or minister. Not even a loaf of bread or a cup of wine in sight.

As an uneasy newlywed, desperate to blend in with and be liked by these virtual strangers I called family, I felt more than a little nervous as I watched all this. The part of me that questioned the very

existence of God went to war with the shreds of my remaining childhood faith. As uncertain as I was about what I believed, I knew without question that holding church in a backyard just a few feet from the
port-a-potty rented for the weekend, with Cousin Tony ministering
from the picnic-table pulpit—*unordained* Cousin Tony, in his Polo
shirt, khaki shorts, and flip-flops, for heaven's sake—was wrong, if not
downright blasphemous.

This isn't real church, I thought to myself. *Real church is supposed to
be in a church. Obviously.* I was accustomed to the Masses of my childhood, of course, which were performed indoors, with a priest and
communion and pews. Masses to which I'd worn my very best patent
leather Mary Janes. Not shorts. And certainly not flip-flops. Occasionally when I was growing up I encountered one of those contemporary
parishes, the ones that broke out the guitars and tambourines, a long-
haired woman in a flowy skirt harmonizing an Amy Grant song. But
that was as out-of-the-box as it got. Once I attended a Mass in the
Florida Keys during which the priest's cocker spaniel stepped jauntily
with him down the aisle. But that was the Keys. Never had I experienced church beneath a rent-a-tent; never in someone's backyard at a
weekend barbeque; and absolutely never with a family member serving as minister.

I watched Tony set a boom box on the picnic table "altar" and realized with horror that I was going to be forced to fumble my way
through the lyrics of "Amazing Grace" without the benefit of a thundering organ to obscure the fact that I knew only half of the first verse.
I considered fleeing to Aunt Carolyn's bathroom and hiding among
the rumpled hand towels, but I didn't want to suggest I was too good
for this kind of church. So I settled into a creaking lawn chair and

mumbled along with the boom box. Everyone else was clearly relaxed and casual—Cousin Paul even munched a doughnut hole during the service—while I stared at my feet, murmured the Lord's Prayer, and stuttered my way through the unfamiliar hymns. Finally, after an agonizing half hour, we sang a closing song, and it was mercifully done. The Haukebos rearranged the chairs for lunch, and we ate grilled bratwurst and cheesy potato hotdish.

The backyard church service felt awkward and unfamiliar that first summer and for several summers after. Each year I dreaded the moment on Sunday morning when Brad's family would begin to arrange the lawn chairs in rows under the tent. I knew what was coming, and I was always self-conscious and uncomfortable as I stood in the back, mouthing the words to prayers and hymns, my husband's arm encircling my waist. But as time went on, I also began to experience something new and unsettling on those hot July mornings under the tent: I began to feel a yearning. I began to want to be part of what the Haukebos so clearly had. I couldn't quite put my finger on it, but as I glanced from Brad to his mom and dad and his aunts, uncles, and cousins all gathered in the shade beneath the tent, I sensed they had a kind of comfort, peace, and security that eluded me. I sensed that while I was lost, they had somehow, inexplicably, been found.

———

As I began to attend Lutheran church services with greater regularity, I discovered, to my surprise, that I missed many aspects of Catholic Mass, especially the elements of mystery and ritual. As far as I could tell, the Lutheran church was about as mysterious as a loaf of Wonder

Bread. The Catholic Masses I remembered, on the other hand, were nothing short of a spectacle.

Steeped in ancient history and solemn ritual, Mass captivated me, from the font of holy water trickling in the back of the church to the ornate chalice, housed in the glittering tabernacle adjacent to the altar. As a kid I thought the tabernacle was actually the house of God, literally his house, where he lived as a miniature version of himself, with tiny tables, chairs, and a bed, and a couple of diminutive angels in there to bring him tea and play the occasional game of Go Fish. My sister, on the other hand, insisted the priest was God and the altar boys his angels. My mom tried to set her straight one day, but Jeanine would have none of it. "Of course that's God and his angels," she explained to my mother. "Why else would they be dressed that way?" she asked, referring to the priest's richly embroidered vestments and the altar boys' shin-length white gowns.

When I was young we attended Saint Joseph's, a tiny church nestled into the Italian neighborhood of my town. I loved driving through that area, all the houses dripping with adornment: lavish tiered fountains splashing in the front yard and often lit with a pink spotlight at night; the obligatory Mary shrine draped in plastic ivy garlands; ceramic gnomes frolicking amid the scraggly grass. The Italians went all out at Christmas, their houses, shrubs, trees, and even mailboxes wrapped in a blinking blitz of lights, a cardboard crèche center stage in the floodlight's beam. The manger was always empty until Christmas morning, and then suddenly baby Jesus would appear, nestled into his cardboard crib.

Saint Joseph's was different from the other Catholic churches I'd attended—namely because it was a basement. It was rumored the founding members ran out of money about a third of the way through construction. Instead of calling it quits entirely, they slapped a roof on the basement and pronounced it a done deal. To enter the church we walked down a flight of cement stairs and through a set of wooden doors, which opened into the nave. The sanctuary consisted of about twenty rows of pews arranged on a green linoleum floor leading to the altar. My dad called it Saint Hole in the Ground.

Aside from the fact that we attended church in a cellar each week, everything else about Saint Joseph's was in line with tradition, including the funeral Masses. Every detail of the service was drenched in meaning and purpose, from the pungent incense leaking out of the clanking censer over the casket to the holy water, shaken like a baby rattle over the mourners. As the droplets rained onto bowed heads, I would crane my neck, stand on tiptoe, and plead silently, *Hit me! Hit me!*—anticipating the warm splash of water on my forehead or cheek. *Come on come on come on,* I would beg, confident that a smidge of holy water would cure all my ills.

I also loved the font of holy water positioned near the entrance of every Catholic church. Sometimes it was a free-standing bowl, but more often it was a humble niche carved into the stone wall, like a soap dish, holding a shallow pool of water. I loved to walk into the church's dim dampness on a roasting August day, dip my fingers into the cool water, and lightly dab my forehead, chest, and shoulders in the sign of the cross. Once, as a gift, I received a tiny vial of holy water that had come directly from the Vatican. I doled it out in infinitesimal droplets over a period of years, always gauging whether a prayer warranted a drop of the precious water to give it a little more oomph. Occasionally I was tempted to dump the entire contents of the vial over my head to see if I would be magically transformed in some way, but I could never actually bring myself to do it. I was worried about the droplets that might not be absorbed into my hair, since holy water is not allowed to splash onto the ground or swirl down the drain. Like any other sacramental item, holy water requires proper disposal, which means pouring it into a hole dug into the ground, preferably in a spot that will not be walked upon later.

When I first started to attend the Lutheran church, I was keenly aware of what was missing. The services seemed lackluster compared to the mystery, ritual, and formality of a Catholic Mass. I missed the routines, such as genuflecting toward the altar before settling into the pew and making the sign of the cross after I'd dipped my fingers into the holy water—rituals that had grounded and comforted me in their familiarity and repetition. Once I grew accustomed to the less fancy format, though, I began to notice something else about the Lutheran church service that was different: Jesus seemed to be the center of attention.

This will sound crazy (and please understand, this was my perception of Mass as a child—I am by no means declaring that this is what the Catholic church is really about), but as I recall, when I was growing up, Jesus didn't seem to be the focus of Mass. There was the gospel reading, the consecration, and the rite of communion, of course, and I'm sure he must have made an appearance in the Christmas and Easter sermons—after all, it's difficult to get through the entire Advent season without mentioning baby Jesus and the manger and the cows lowing and all that—but typically Jesus was the not the focus of the priest's homily. Instead we heard about sweet Mary, the array of saints, the creepy devil, and the amorphous God.

Protestants have long insisted that Catholics place a little too much emphasis on Mary, but as a kid, I was glad for her reassuring and comforting presence. I related to her because Mary was accessible; not only was she a mother—kind, albeit slightly aloof—but she was human, like me. We learned about Mary in catechism class, prayed the Hail Mary, and asked for her intercession in a shrine surrounded by flickering candles. Many Catholic churches have one—a statue of Mary standing willowy and robed in an alcove adjacent to the altar, staring benevolently at baby Jesus in her arms, row upon row of votive candles glowing at her feet. Standing at the foot of Mary under her kind, unwavering gaze, I felt secure and protected.

Along with Mary we also had the saints, dozens of them. We prayed intercessory prayers to specific saints depending on our needs. If you lost your watch or favorite Smurf figurine, for example, you would pray a novena (nine prayers for nine consecutive days) to Saint Anthony, the patron saint of lost items. If you faced a desperate situation, like an upcoming algebra exam, you would pray to Saint Jude, the saint of hopeless causes. Saint Joseph was a particular favorite among homeowners, as he was the saint you called upon before putting your house on the market. My sister and I were fascinated by the story my mom told of a relative who buried a statue of Saint Joseph, head down, near the For Sale sign in the front yard. Within days of the saint's entombment, the home sold.

Unfortunately, looming in the background and casting a deep shadow over Mary and all the saints was always the devil. Satan was the main character, the evil protagonist. I swear sometimes it seemed as though Satan got more airtime during Mass than God himself. The devil was pretty much the central theme, the main topic. I don't recall hearing much about love, forgiveness, and grace in church when I was growing up, but I sure understood sin and shame, guilt and punishment. I wasn't taught how to act as a good Christian, but I was certainly drilled on how *not* to behave. Mix generous helpings of shame, guilt, and fear and hang the devil over my head, and basically what I got was hell.

The God I remember from my childhood was an authoritative and powerful God, at times even vengeful, punishing, and unpredictable. He was impressive and commanding, certainly, but loving? caring? concerned for me personally? I never got that impression. My God was too distant and vast to be caring, loving, and compassionate as well.

I laughed recently when my friend Andrea told me about her childhood God, one who sounded remarkably like Zeus, moving his humans like pawns on the chessboard. Andrea recalled that if she made fun of her younger brother or gave him a shove, and then a minute later stubbed her toe on the coffee table, her mother was sure to point out, "Well, what did you expect? God is punishing you for being mean to your brother." Andrea's God was even worse than mine. Andrea's God schemed against her.

As an adult looking back, what seems most strange to me about the church hierarchy wasn't so much who played the starring role, but who was missing. God was omniscient, omnipotent, and omnipresent, sort of like Santa Claus but a lot less predictable. The devil labored tirelessly to tempt me. And Mary and the saints were human, persevering right there in the trenches. So where, then, did that leave Jesus? Suspended on the cross above my head, his head crowned in thorns, his face, depending on the depiction, either contorted in agony or placidly serene. Jesus was present in that he was literally hanging over my head on the cross, but he was alarmingly absent in almost every other way. Sure, I came across him in the gospel readings. Sure, I celebrated his birth in the humble manger and his resurrection on Easter. Sure, I vaguely gave thanks for his body and blood and his sacrifice for me during communion. But other than that, it seemed he was hardly mentioned. The priests' sermons more often focused on lofty theological musings, the lure of Satan's temptations, or the power of sin. If Jesus *was* mentioned at great length, it was usually to expound on his agony and great suffering, which only intensified my guilt, instead of offering an opportunity to be thankful for his loving sacrifice. I'm sure, as a child, I gravitated toward and was more inclined to remember the more "exciting" sermons about the devil and hell, but still, I rarely recall a priest speaking much about Jesus's love or compassion; nor do I remember the priest connecting Jesus's love for us with his death on the cross. From my childhood all the way until adulthood, Jesus was a nonentity, an archetype rather than a real presence.

It wasn't until I began to attend Lutheran services off and on with Brad in Connecticut that Jesus began to show up in church in a memorable way. At Ebenezer, Pastor Cheryl always linked Jesus with love—that was all we ever heard about: Jesus and love, Jesus and love. I figured it was because she was earthy-crunchy; I thought that was her thing: love, grace, and Jesus. I assumed Pastor Cheryl just had a unique feel-good take on religion.

But then we moved to Nebraska, and Jesus began to crop up everywhere—from the neighbor who tagged her Halloween candy with a Jesus message to the mothers I met in playgroup who talked about God and Jesus and the churches they attended. It was only after we began to visit Southwood Lutheran—the church we eventually joined—and I continuously heard the same message—love and grace and Jesus, love and grace and Jesus—that I began to realize perhaps Jesus played a bigger role in the Christian faith.

I remember vividly the day we attended Southwood's new-member orientation. Brad and I sat through an overview of Luther and his Ninety-Five Theses and a few details about the sacraments in Lutheranism (only two, piece of cake!). The class went smoothly, but then, just as I was gathering my purse and coat, the pastor asked us to join him in song to close out the class. "Let's sing 'Jesus Loves Me,'" he suggested. Right on cue, twenty brand-new members joined him, singing lyrics as familiar and comforting as "Twinkle, Twinkle, Little Star."

I stood there rigid and dumbfounded, silently moving my lips while everyone around me belted out the lyrics memorized from their earliest days in Sunday school: "Jesus loves me, this I know. For the Bible tells me so..." I didn't know the words. I didn't even recognize the tune. I stood there with my purse and coat clutched in my hands, fake-singing, a smile plastered on my face. I was certain everyone knew the truth: that I was a fake, a fraud, a lying Lutheran, a pseudo-believer among real Christians.

I didn't blame the pastor. For everyone else in the room, singing "Jesus Loves Me" was clearly a good thing. The beloved childhood song offered them a connection, a unifying thread, common ground. But as I pretended to mouth the words to the unfamiliar song, I knew I didn't belong.

Even more bizarre than fake-singing "Jesus Loves Me" was the fact that, when the orientation was over, I was, as far as everyone else was concerned, a certified Lutheran. "That's it?" I asked Brad in disbelief. "I don't have to go through some sort of training or get baptized or officially convert? I don't even have to sign anything?" Once again, I was thrust out of my comfort zone. Where were the rules and rituals? Where was the complicated system of repentance? What about confession? Who was even in charge? As far as I was concerned, Lutheranism was Catholicism stripped to the bare bones. All that was left was baptism, communion, and lots of talk about Jesus, love, and grace.

Slowly it dawned on me: this Jesus-love theme was not a fluke; this was *it,* the main topic, the big theme. Jesus wasn't just the subplot; he and his love were the story around which everything revolved.

Honestly, I didn't know what to do with that. This Jesus—real, living, and present—was new to me. This wasn't Jesus as a baby, a doll wrapped in swaddling clothes and placed in a rustic manger on the altar on Christmas day. This wasn't Jesus suspended over my head on the cross as a symbol of forgiveness. Southwood's ministers seemed to present a different Jesus than the one I knew at arm's length, and they seemed to suggest that I ought to connect with this Jesus as a real, relatable presence in my everyday life.

While this presentation of Jesus appealed to me—after all, what's not to like about a loving, relatable Jesus?—it also intimidated me. Clearly I didn't have that kind of relationship with Jesus. Clearly I didn't have *any* relationship with Jesus. And clearly I was the only one. All the Lutherans lining the pews each Sunday morning seemed to get it. They knew all the words to the song, so to speak, while I was left lip-syncing in the last row.

Why Not?

The soul should always stand
ajar, ready to welcome the
ecstatic experience.
—EMILY DICKINSON

One Sunday, a couple of years into my sporadic churchgoing, I
listened from my usual seat in the very last pew as the pastor
introduced a new sermon series he called "Just Walk Across the Room."
Pastor Greg suggested that the church's members should reach out to
those in search of answers and help guide them toward God. He called
them "irreligious people," these lost and wandering ones.

As I heard Pastor Greg talk about these people's needs, I realized
he was talking about me. *How ironic,* I thought. The pastor was urging his congregants to embrace irreligious people—the "other," the
outsider, the person on the fringe—yet *I* was the "other," an irreligious
person sitting right there in the church pew. *I am lost, but maybe, just*

maybe, I thought, as I sat in the back pew with my arms folded over my chest, *there's hope for me.*

At the time I was seeing a therapist for counseling—a therapist who was a member of the same church—and often during our weekly sessions we would talk about faith and religion. She knew my faith history, and she also knew I'd been attending church on and off for a couple of years. "I think you should make an appointment to talk to Pastor Greg," she suggested one day.

I balked. "Why would I do that? What do I possibly have to say to Pastor Greg?" I couldn't think of anything worse than going to talk to a minister in his office. How creepy and weird and uncomfortable.

"I think you'd be surprised," my counselor said. "I think it would be good for you." She didn't hound me, but she didn't let the matter entirely drop either. Every couple of weeks or so, my counselor would ask the same question: "So. Have you made that appointment with Pastor Greg yet?"

After the "Just Walk Across the Room" sermon that morning, I went home, sat at the computer, and banged out an e-mail to Pastor Greg before I lost my nerve. I didn't hem and haw. I didn't mull over my words. I just did it.

"Dear Pastor Greg," I typed.

> I really enjoyed your sermon this morning, and it struck home in a deeply personal way. I think it's interesting that while you were urging Southwood's members to seek out lost souls, you probably didn't expect that a person wouldn't have to look further than herself. But that's true for me. I am what you

termed today "irreligious." I'm a bit of a lost soul. But your
sermon prompted me to write this e-mail, to ask whether
you'd be willing to meet sometime, at your convenience,
for a conversation. Thank you for your consideration. I look
forward to hearing from you.

And then, before I could change my mind, I hit Send.

So of course Pastor Greg invited me for a one-on-one conversation. Believe me, I tried to get out of it. I thought about calling the
church office and saying I was sick, feigning horrible stomach cramps
or strep throat. But I was far too superstitious to rely on the faux illness
excuse. I figured once I claimed I was barfing or writhing on the floor
in intestinal distress, I'd soon be struck down with illness in reality. So
I went.

Walking into that room was worse than confession. At least in the
confessional you have the cover of darkness. This conversation took
place face to face in the light of day, Pastor Greg and I sitting in metal
folding chairs, a rickety table between us. And although Pastor Greg
attempted to put me at ease with a bit of small talk, I figured it wouldn't
get any easier until I explained, or at least tried to explain, why I was
there. So I took the plunge. I drew in a deep breath and launched "the
conversation," taking my usual circuitous approach. "Well, I'm at what
you'd call square one," I suggested cryptically and then began to offer
glimpses of my doubt in dribbles.

The conversation meandered like this for a while until finally,
after about twenty minutes of getting nowhere, Pastor Greg asked
bluntly, "So what exactly *do* you believe?"

I hesitated. And then finally, for the first time ever, I told the truth: "Well, honestly, I'm not too sure I believe in God. Actually sometimes I feel more like I don't believe in God than I do."

The funny thing was, nothing happened. The earth didn't stop spinning, the church pillars didn't crumble, Pastor Greg didn't even grimace. In fact he acted as if this was not new information, as though he had heard this one before, that maybe he had even heard worse. And his response was kind and compassionate. "I believe that God is with you, that the Holy Spirit is working within you and has brought you here today," he said simply. "I believe that's evidence that you're not as far lost as you think you are."

I wasn't sure how to respond to that. I couldn't say what I really felt, which was that I thought he was full of baloney. So I told him a half truth: that I felt hopeful, that his confidence in me, in the Holy Spirit working in me, gave me hope. I wasn't falling on my knees in a trembling Saint Paul–like conversion, but amid the darkness of my doubt I felt a glimmer, a faint spark of hope. I actually felt something stir inside, a breath of excitement, of possibility. I had finally admitted outright to someone, a religious authority no less, that I had doubts, big doubts, questions, and fears, and that person told me it was okay. I had confessed my darkest sin—that I lacked true, heartfelt faith—and instead of a gasp of horror, I received only compassion, comfort, and above all, hope.

Truthfully, a Saint Paul–like conversion would have been a heck of a lot easier. What's not to like about falling over in the middle of the road, hearing the voice of God bellowing loud and clear from the heavens, and then dusting oneself off and resuming life as a convicted believer? It's quick, it's obvious, and there's no room for questioning or doubt. But that was not the kind of conversion I got. What I got instead was, as Methodism's founder John Wesley described it, a "heart strangely warmed."[1]

It's said that while listening to a reading of Martin Luther's preface to the book of Romans, Wesley experienced a faint stirring, a strange feeling he described as a warming of his heart, which, he later said, enabled him to make the leap to trusting Jesus for his salvation. While Wesley went on to do great things with his strangely warmed heart, it wasn't exactly a lightning strike. It wasn't a Paul-on-the-road-to-Damascus moment. Personally I was looking for something a little more dramatic, something undeniable and unquestionable, something more than a slow, subtle warming of the heart. Wesley's experience sounded like turning the oven on to two hundred degrees and heating up Thanksgiving leftovers on Friday afternoon. I was looking for the entire house to burn down. I wanted a miracle of biblical proportions.

Miracles are everywhere in the Bible. A stark raving madman witnesses his demons funnel into a herd of pigs. People rise from the dead and start doing jumping jacks. Peter walks on water. Paul falls down blind in the middle of the road and stands up converted. *If miracles were so prevalent in the Bible,* I wondered, *why can't one happen to me? Couldn't I be jogging along the trail in Lincoln, be struck blind (just for a few minutes, please; three days isn't necessary), and hear the thundering voice of God?* I was a good candidate for a miraculous conversion, so why didn't I get one? Why didn't I get a clear sign, a dramatic moment? Probably because I would have assumed I'd gone completely bonkers.

Maybe it was the two years of erratic church attendance and hearing the consistent repetition of the "love and grace" message that finally began to turn my heart. Maybe it was the weekly conversations with my counselor. Maybe it was the faint spark of hope I'd felt after my conversation with Pastor Greg. Maybe he'd been right and it *was* the Holy Spirit at work. I can't point to one single dramatic catalyst that prompted my heart to begin warming to the concept of belief. All I know is that it began, not long after my meeting with Pastor Greg, with one simple question: *Why not?*

Over a period of weeks I began to turn this new question around in my mind. Simply, why not? For many years I hadn't allowed myself to think about belief or unbelief at all. Then, when I finally began to accept my lack of faith, I was never willing to suspend my unbelief, even for a moment, to see what it felt like. I never gave myself the opportunity, the option, to believe.

So when I did—when sometime after that meeting with Pastor Greg I cracked open the window just wide enough to ask that simple question, "Why not?"—it felt, as C. S. Lewis once said, as if I were loosening a stiff corset or unbuckling a suit of armor.[2] I began to ask myself the question every day, again and again: *Why not? Why can't God exist? Why can't there be a heaven? Why can't Jesus have been the Savior, sent to save us? Sent to save me? Why not?*

Asking "Why not?" loosened a single button on the tightly cinched corset. Asking "Why not?" unclasped a single buckle on my impenetrable suit of armor. Asking "Why not?" was a gentle relaxing of my strict black-and-white take on faith, just enough to throw the whole equation ever so slightly off balance.

One morning, shortly after I had begun to ask myself "Why not?"

again and again, I experienced one of my infamous "I'm just not cut out to have kids" moments. It began routinely, with Noah and Rowan erupting into sidesplitting giggles, one screaming, "Bum!" the other responding, "Underwear!" "Poop!" "Penis!" back and forth, on and on, over their Eggo French Toaster Sticks. Some days I am actually able to ignore the potty talk; they are boys after all, and this is what boys do. This particular morning, though, was not such a day.

"That's enough!" I declared in my Mommy's-about-to-lose-it voice pinched shrilly through clenched teeth. They paid me no heed. "That's it! I've had it! I'm serious!" I yelled. "No treats! You've lost dessert, both of you, for the entire day!" This got results. Loss of dessert was big; it was serious, and it was my way of saying, "Mommy's the Boss; don't you dare mess with me."

The downside of dessert retraction, however, was the inevitable tsunami of wailing it provoked. As the situation quickly escalated to DEFCON 1—with tears, stomping, sobbing, the whole bit—I lost it. Totally and completely lost it. The kind of premeditated losing it where you run around the house slamming down open windows so you can let loose without the fear of neighbors hearing and dialing Child Protective Services.

Ranting and raving, I ordered the boys to their rooms, dragging one not so gently by an arm and depositing him on his rug and carrying the other on my hip sideways like a forty-pound sack of Yukon Golds. Doors slammed, the wailing reached the fevered pitch of lemurs in heat, and I joined in, shutting myself in my room, weeping pathetically and chanting again and again like a gouged CD, "PleaseGodpleaseGodpleaseGodhelpmehelpmehelpme."

Sixty seconds later my bedroom door creaked open slowly, and in came Noah, calm, serene, his big eyes dark and round like a baby seal's. He perched next to me on the edge of the bed and leaned his head on my shoulder. And that was it. He didn't say anything, didn't hug me, whine, beg for love, chew me out for being a sucky mother. He just sat quietly and rested, a simple gesture but one that exuded all the right things—love, forgiveness, and peace.

It was, I knew instantly, a gesture from God. What better conduit than my own firstborn son, the person who loved me most in the world, one of the three people I loved most in the world. God had answered my desperate prayer; God had spoken to me through my own son.

Then my rational side kicked in. *Yeah…whatever; it's just a coincidence,* I thought to myself. *He's just being nice because he thinks I've gone off the deep end for real this time.*

Almost as instantly as my heart told me I had experienced a blessing, a connection with God, my head squashed such a preposterous idea. But even as I picked up the pieces of my life and reassembled something close to normalcy for the remainder of the day, I couldn't help but think, *Maybe, just maybe.* I couldn't help but wonder, *Why not?* I could not shake the feeling that the incident was something more than coincidence, something more than a mere fluke.

It wasn't easy for me to choose blessing over coincidence that day, and it's still not. After twenty years of unbelief, doubt had become a habit. Doubting was easy, routine; it was my natural, instinctive reaction. Somewhere along the line I had stopped considering any other options. Doubt was my default. So choosing the blessing, the miracle, over coincidence had to be a conscious choice. I had to dismiss doubt as the crutch that it was, dismiss my gut instinct and embrace the more challenging alternative.

Choosing blessing and rejecting doubt is still a conscious choice I make every day. Some days I am more successful than others. But in the end I always go back to the "Why not?" revelation. The afternoon of the meltdown incident I asked myself, *Why not? Why couldn't it have been God answering my insane prayer? Why couldn't he have been bestowing a blessing, sending down a miracle in Noah? Why not?*

I've been asking "Why not?" ever since.

———

If we're honest with ourselves, I suspect a lot of us are looking for the big, flashy miracle—the billboard moment when everything is crystal clear and all doubts are washed away for good, the media-worthy miracle that makes the evening news. I know that's what I want. I find myself thinking, *If only God could give me one clear sign, if only he would come down and do a miracle, then I would believe 100 percent for sure. If I got a clear sign, I wouldn't have any more doubts.* But I'm not so sure that's the only way God operates. I'm beginning to think he gives us these ordinary miracles, these small blessings, these "Why not?" moments in the midst of the everyday instead, so we will learn to open our eyes and see him not just in the wild, over-the-top, media-worthy miracles, but in the hundreds of everyday miracles as well.

The truth is, once I began to question my doubts at least as much as I questioned my toddler-step, doddering faith, I began to see small miracles everywhere.

One day while watering the garden I heard Noah yell: "Quick, Mommy! Come here! Come here! Hurry!" His voice was urgent, pressing, so much so that I stopped what I was doing and quickly walked over to where he was crouched at the curb. I bent down next to him, concerned that something was the matter, but he just pointed into the air.

Floating on a gentle current along the tops of the phlox was a curious bug, a miniscule creature about a quarter the size of my pinkie nail. It looked to me like a thin shred of paper, the handmade kind—bumpy, lumpy, pasty paper with bits of flower petals and leaves rolled into it. The creature bobbed along the bee balm for a bit and then floated over to Noah and Rowan, navigating its linty body between them, as if to take a closer look at their big bobble heads. Rowan named the bug Klee Klee because it looked like the teeniest shred of Kleenex. We sat on the curb next to the flower garden and marveled at the insect as it gracefully inched over the mountainous folds of Rowan's T-shirt, its snow-white wings wispy and ragged.

I would never have noticed this delicate creature on my own, so bent was I on watering the drooping coneflower and deadheading the bee balm, wrenching the ivy's suffocating grip off the phlox and pulling the weeds. But Noah had insisted I look, squealing and bellowing so persistently I was forced to tune in, if only to quiet the racket. And when I did I was overwhelmed with gratitude and awe.

I began to wonder, *What if?* What if *these* were the blessings, the miracles—these ordinary happenings in ordinary life? Why not? Maybe, I mused, the blessings had been right here all along, right under my nose. Maybe God didn't swoop in with the mighty and dramatic moments—the lightning and the earthquakes and the winds—but instead floated in gently, softly, on the wings of a Klee Klee. I've always lived too fast, too furiously, too frenetically. I needed to be forced to slow down, and that is exactly what Noah and Rowan did—and still do. They slow me down, they point the way, they encourage me to notice God's gifts. My children give me opportunities to see God, to hear him, feel him, and look for him in the quiet and the chaos of the everyday.

Slowly I began to realize that it is these beautifully ordinary experiences that comprise the most intimate fabric of life, ordinary life that is extraordinary in so many ways.

When my nephew Oliver was born I traveled back to Massachusetts to meet him and to help my sister adjust to the early days of parenting. I spent most of my four-day visit walking with Oliver, because, as you probably know, when you have a new baby, you walk. You walk through dinnertime, swaying in front of the television while the rest of the family feasts on lasagna. You walk outside, the sawing cicadas buzzing into the dusk as you circle the scorched grass in the backyard. You walk at three in the morning, the television muted, the local real estate channel flickering grainy photos of condos and townhouses. You walk and walk and walk.

I clearly remember what a finely tuned *process* it was just to sit as a new mother. After spending thirty minutes or so bobbing and swaying Noah to sleep, I would approach the couch and begin to lower myself gingerly, slowly down. And it never failed. Just as my bottom grazed the sofa, just as my muscles ever so slightly relaxed into the cushions,

Noah would spring into action, flailing and howling in protest. It had all been a ruse. He may have looked like he was sleeping, his mouth drooping into the shape of a delicate O, but as soon as I even partially relaxed my limbs into the folds of the couch, the prefuss cough would commence, followed almost immediately by a full-blown roar, his wrinkled little face indignant. And then the swaying and the bobbing and the walking would begin anew.

That's why I was surprised to find I actually enjoyed walking Oliver. Apparently enough time had elapsed since my own kids were infants that I was finally able to savor the experience. My job was to placate Oliver after Jeanine had nursed him during the night so she could sleep in between feedings. Oliver was typically fussy after nursing, so we figured I could soothe him during the nighttime shifts while Jeanine caught up on some sleep.

On one such night, I decided to walk Oliver outside, figuring at the very least he would be out of Jeanine's and Matt's earshot. I wrestled him into the sling, cinching the football-field length of fabric as snugly over my shoulder as I could. Oliver screamed in the driveway, squeezing his eyes shut against the automatic floodlight over the garage, his face mad and remarkably troll-like. "Shhhhhh. Shhhhh. Shhhh. Okay. Okay. Okay, keep your shorts on," I shushed him, irritated with my inadequacy but clearly trying to blame it on him. The minute I started down the driveway, though, he quieted, and before I reached the end of the street, Oliver was asleep. I had forgotten about that tendency, how a baby often reaches a crescendo of crabbiness before crashing into slumber, a dramatic release of pent-up stress and anxiety before the peace descends.

Oliver bobbed rhythmically against my thigh. My palm cupped

his tiny head through the sling fabric, protecting it from the bumping as I strolled around the block. The night was beautiful, languid and humid, a slight breeze rustling the oak leaves high above my head. I wore my pajamas, a pair of pink-striped lounge pants and a tank top. The *thwap, thwap, thwap* of my flip-flops against my heels mingled with the noise of the neighbors laughing and talking excitedly over one another in Spanish. A crackling bonfire in their backyard fire pit tossed sparks into the blackness, and Latin music, trumpets and trombones, brassy and festive, drifted with the breeze to the far side of the neighborhood, a little bit louder, then fainter again. Oliver slept. I tucked my free hand under his warm back and felt his heartbeat flutter.

In those moments with Oliver, I experienced everything I feared I had missed with my own kids. With Noah and Rowan I had been so caught up in the routines and the rules, the shoulds and shouldn'ts, what this book or that website recommended, I missed the babies themselves, their whole infancy. *Is he sleeping too long? Why isn't he sleeping longer? Should he be sleeping in bed with us? Should I let him cry it out? Should we Ferberize him? Am I feeding him enough? Should I introduce the bottle? Will the pacifier cause nipple confusion?* I didn't live their infancy, I didn't experience it, I didn't soak it up. I merely managed it.

What a thing to regret, that you missed your babies' babyhood.

When I later mentioned this regret to Brad, he insisted I was wrong. He recalled many evenings when I had dozed with Noah on the living room couch, dusk falling early as Brad sizzled stir-fry on the stove. I remember it too, but dimly, fuzzily, as if I observed the scene through a frosted window rather than from the inside, living the moment.

My late-night walk with Oliver felt real, though, and I was grateful for that. Maybe I was able to cherish Oliver more fully because I knew the opportunity was fleeting. After all, he lived more than fifteen hundred miles from me. I knew I would only see him once, maybe twice a year, so I had to soak up his lovely babyness while I could. The transitory nature of the moment allowed me to experience it more deeply, more authentically. The very fact that the moment wouldn't last, the fact that it was not a permanent commitment, allowed me to relinquish the questions, anxieties, and fears.

Or perhaps it was due to a distance of another sort, an emotional distance. Oliver was not mine. He was not my child, therefore I could love him unencumbered and unburdened, liberated from the pressing responsibility of his livelihood and life. I didn't have to worry about the shoulds and shouldn'ts, the websites and the books. All that mattered was nestling him close to me and feeling his warm lightness on my chest. It must be how grandparents feel, this freedom to love with abandon, this love completely unchained from gnawing anxiety.

It also crossed my mind that the feeling I relished with Oliver that night was something different altogether. Maybe our walk together was simply a gift from God, a reminder, a wake-up call. Noah and Rowan were young yet. It wasn't too late. There was still so much left to enjoy, so many more opportunities to love with abandon. The magic in the walking, in the Klee Klees, in ordinary life, was still available, waiting to be noticed and celebrated.

———

As I noticed more and more of these ordinary miracles in my life, I began to wonder if perhaps God operates that way intentionally. Perhaps there's a reason he doesn't go with the big, splashy miracles like Fourth of July fireworks in the sky. I started to suspect that my grasping toward a belief in God was a little bit like my experiences of swimming.

I learned to swim in a lake at Sun Valley, the campground where my family spent our summers. It was a small lake, a pond really, its water so murky my toes looked tangerine in two feet of water. They disappeared altogether as I waded up to my thighs. While swimming out to the raft, I would open my eyes underwater to a velvety green, the sun shooting shafts of sparkling chartreuse through the haze. The color of the water changed like a chameleon, brown if it had rained the night before, emerald in the humid August days.

Sometimes I dolphin-dived straight down, swimming through layer after layer of deepening green until I reached the cold bottom, the water colored dusky black. I would graze my fingers across the gravel, lingering there for a moment before the chill prevailed. Then, pushing off the rocks with my toes, I'd thrust to the surface like a torpedo.

Most of the lake floor was comprised of sand and stone, but occasionally I would hit a mucky spot, soft and oozy. A big patch of mud, squishy with decomposed leaves, lay at the base of the dock where we had our swimming lessons. Hunky lifeguard Pete would sink a plastic milk jug filled with sand, and each of us would dive down to the bottom, grope around in the darkness, and then lug it one-handed to the bright surface, legs scissoring, bubbles streaming from our noses like otters. The murky water didn't bother me as a kid. But as I got older, I developed a distrust of what I couldn't see lurking beneath the surface.

One summer when Brad and I were still dating we canoed a lake up in the Boundary Waters, a remote, uninhabited wilderness in northern Minnesota. It was an unnaturally hot afternoon, with the sun glinting off the motionless water and the aluminum canoe hot to the touch. When we took a break, dragging the canoe halfway up the pebbly beach, Brad stripped off his T-shirt and jumped off the rocky point into the cold water. "It's great!" he yelled, treading about fifteen feet out. "Come on! Jump in!"

"I don't know," I said, standing in my sports bra and shorts on the rock, the moss spongy under my feet. "I'm kind of cooled off already. I may skip it."

"What? Seriously? Oh come on…it's great!" Brad cajoled.

I paused. "Okay, so I have the creeps, all right?" I yelled back, then sheepishly added, "I'm afraid of dead bodies!"

It took Brad a few seconds to digest this information before he yelled his reply: "Well, honey, I can assure you with 100 percent confidence that there are no dead bodies in this lake. No one is here. We're fifty miles from the Canadian border in the middle of nowhere. No dead bodies."

So I jumped in, one of those wimpy half-leaps where you start whirling your hands and arms in circles immediately upon contact with the water so that your head doesn't actually dip beneath the surface. Then I scrambled toward the rock, but not before my foot brushed something slimy and hard. I screamed, the blood-curdling screech echoing throughout the vast expanse of water and pine trees. Brad rolled his eyes when I insisted my foot had brushed a dead body. He swam toward shore and poked his toes around the dead body area, finally concluding wearily that it was nothing more than a submerged tree limb. "Yeah well, whatever. It felt gross," I said, wringing out my hair and turning my face toward the sun.

When I thought about it, these lake-water images struck me as the perfect metaphor for my tentative floundering toward belief. In matters of spirituality I often assumed that if only I knew for sure, if I firmly grasped the answers to all the questions, if I saw clearly how it would all turn out, then I would be okay. I thought if I could see under the surface of that murky water, glimpse what was hidden beneath, my faith would finally be secure, rock solid and steady. On the other hand, my memory of yet another lake experience left me wondering if even that kind of clarity would satisfy.

One summer my family vacationed at a cottage on Silver Lake in New Hampshire. My dad's best friend, Wayne, and his wife, Nancy, owned the humble summer house, which perched on a wooded, rocky hill across the road from the lake. It was rustic, even by my family's Sun Valley camper standards, with a slanted screened porch, lumpy armchairs covered in goldenrod upholstery, and end tables stacked high with back issues of *National Geographic,* the covers crinkled with age and dried water rings. I distinctly remember the smell of the place, musty and vaguely sweet, like old books.

Jeanine and I loved it there, namely because Nancy and Wayne's two daughters were staying at the cottage too. At twelve and ten we idolized Leslie and Paige. Leslie, the oldest, was aloof; I spied on her as she sat in a lounge chair on the dock reading *Seventeen,* one dangling foot skimming the water's surface. But Paige was still young enough for fun. Together we cannonballed off the end of the dock, captured tadpoles among the cattails, and played hide-and-seek in the dim, buggy woods.

The first time I swam from the end of the boat dock to the raft twenty-five feet out, I panicked, thrashing and gasping as I half crawled, half drowned my way to the float. When I finally pulled my-self onto the raft and lay like a glassy-eyed trout on my side, I looked up to see Paige staring down at me, bewildered disdain written on her face. I'm sure she assumed I was the world's most graceless swimmer, but I didn't tell Paige the reason I had nearly drowned swimming to the raft. I had been terrified. Not by fish or lake weed or images of *Jaws,* but by the shocking clarity of the water.

The water in Silver Lake was so clear you could see forty feet to the bottom. It wasn't until you were sitting in a rocking rowboat one hundred yards out that the bottom of the lake finally faded into blue darker than denim. Standing on the raft shivering in the hot sun, water droplets glistening round bubbles on my Coppertone-oiled skin, I gazed down to the lake bottom. Boulders as big as cars, undulating weeds, even the rusted cable spiraling straight down, anchoring the tipping raft to the lake floor, were so startlingly clear it seemed as though I could reach down and brush them with my fingertips. The sight was so real it looked fake, like I was peering into a tabletop aquarium complete with plastic plants and miniature rocks.

You would think I'd have found Silver Lake's clear water, with all its contents easily identified, comforting. But it was just the opposite, in fact. Something felt off balance. I had too much information, like I was a voyeur peering at a private world while someone or something stared right back at my pale dangling legs and red one-piece Speedo. I felt vulnerable, exposed. All that clarity, all that realness beneath my fluttering feet was too much.

The aquarium clear wasn't so gratifying after all, and I wonder now if faith isn't a little bit similar. I thought I wanted pristine clarity rather than the green murk, mysterious and uncertain. Yet Silver Lake turned out to be too much. The sight of everything right there, clear, defined, visible, was crushing rather than comforting. In fact, when I was younger it was the velvety dim of Sun Valley's lake that enveloped me in cool comfort.

Perhaps God knows this is true for us humans. Maybe he knows the whole enchilada would simply be too much, too overwhelming, too mind boggling. So instead he gives us just enough—the shaft of brilliant light in the murky green, the moment when we realize, "There it is, yes, and it's been there all along." The "Why not?" moment. The ordinary miracle: Noah's eyes serene as he sat on the edge of my bed with his head on my shoulder. Klee Klee floating by the bee balm. A quiet walk with a newborn nephew.

Writer Donald McCullough calls these glimpses—these shafts of chartreuse light in the darkness, these clearly defined snapshots—moments of "abundant life." McCullough says, "Our imagination is too crippled to walk into a new land. But once in a while, even in our broken, death-marked existence, we experience it, unexpectedly and with a force that pulls us out of the grave." McCullough likens these brief visions to a resurrection in a sense, being delivered from self-centeredness and "turned outward toward a spaciousness large enough to include God, other people, and the world around us."[3]

I'd clearly glimpsed these resurrection moments in my everyday, ordinary life, these instances of turning outward from myself toward God, and not long after I read McCullough's words, I experienced another such moment of abundant life, right smack in the middle of the Minneapolis airport, of all places.

I was bound for my grandmother's funeral in Massachusetts, and as we began our final descent into the Twin Cities, I was anxious, knowing I'd have only a few minutes to traverse the entire length of the airport in order to catch my connecting flight. As soon as I had wormed my way off the plane and down the jet bridge, I began a Flo-Jo sprint, determined to cover the marathon distance between Concourses C and F in a record five minutes. Dashing onto the tram, heaving like a Clydesdale, I eyed an elderly lady clinging white-knuckled to the pole. She looked terrified, as if she had just boarded a Japanese bullet train rather than an airport tram.

"F10?" she inquired timidly, as I stared panicked and breathless at my watch. We commiserated about the bad weather and the flight delays as the tram lurched glacially toward F Concourse. When we stepped off the train together, it took only a second for me to realize that I was in a bind. Sweet Elderly Lady absolutely could not keep pace with me. I had yet to hit my full Flo-Jo stride, and there she was, hopping two steps behind me like a sandpiper, purse clutched to her chest, her wrinkled face pinched with anxiety. I stayed with her for a few minutes, I swear I did, but then I weakened. I was, after all, trying to get to my grandmother's funeral. So I turned to her as we stood in the middle of the bustling concourse and laid out my plan: "Okay. I'm going to run ahead and tell the gate agent to hold the plane; I promise I'll make them hold the plane!" She nodded and gasped, her eyes wide like a frightened deer's, and I dashed toward F10.

I missed it, of course. I arrived breathless and flushed, my bra straps practically wrapped around my knees, just as the door to the jet bridge clicked shut. I actually *saw* it close as I staggered to the gate, and it galled me to know that the plane wasn't nearly ready to leave, that passengers were still wriggling free of parkas, heaving duffels into overhead bins, and fishing Grisham out of their totes. And it galled me a little, too, to know that if I had not spent those few minutes puttering along with Sweet Elderly Lady as she fumbled down the concourse, I would have been on that plane, settling into my seat and thinking about the lasagna dinner that awaited me at my parents' house.

The gate agent booked me on the next available flight, departing seven hours—yes, *seven hours*—later. I wanted to reach across the counter, snake my scarf around the agent's skinny gazelle neck, and quietly strangle her. And when Sweet Elderly Lady stumbled up to the counter a full five minutes later, all pale and fragile and glassy-eyed, I wanted to strangle her too. I was so mad and sad and bitter and resentful. I knew I would have to eat a cellophane-wrapped turkey sandwich that undoubtedly harbored Listeria, instead of bubbling hot, cheesy, bacteria-free lasagna homemade by my mom. I was tired and overwhelmed and rattled and exasperated. And it was her fault. Sweet Elderly Lady had ruined everything.

As I leaned hollow chested against the counter, she turned to me. "Thank you, dear. Thank you so much for trying," she said, her eyes brimming. "I was walking as fast as I could to get here, and all I could think was, 'That nice girl will help me.' So thank you for trying."

For the love. When she put it like that, so heartfelt and genuine, I felt wretched, guilty for having mentally lambasted her a mere moment ago, guilty for foisting all the blame on her. My eyes filled at the sight of her, so tired and defeated, her sturdy rubber-soled shoes, her lumpy cardigan, a rosary—a rosary for heaven's sake—clutched in her soft, veiny hands. She looked so vulnerable I nearly wept right there at F10.

We exchanged a few pleasantries, each of us wondering how we would kill seven hours in an airport. And then, as I watched her walk away, it struck me. With a sudden jolt of delight I realized I had seven precious hours to myself. Seven laundry- and vacuum-free hours; seven hours of *People, O,* and *SELF* magazines; seven hours of chocolate-covered cashew clusters; seven hours of Starbucks. Seven hours just for me and my treats and my magazines. Realizing all this in a heady rush, I did a joyful hop right there on Concourse F. The freedom and exhilaration of seven found hours were presented to me like a gift, a gift beautifully embellished with a big, extravagant bow, waiting for me to unwrap and discover what was inside.

I sat in a cozy leather chair, shoes off, feet propped on a table, and watched the airport life stream by, love pouring out of me like a river. I beamed my love and goodness onto all my fellow travelers. The businessman balancing a Pizza Hut box, his cell phone tucked under his baggy turkey neck. The frumpy mom with her linty pants and sugar-fueled kids, straining under the weight of a backpack brimming with sippy cups and lovies and blankets and crayons and pretzels and *Green Eggs and Ham.* The elderly couple moving slowly, delicately down the concourse. The slouchy teenagers with their dangling iPod cords, shuffling a respectable distance behind their highly embarrassing parents. The skinny girl in her filmy dress and UGGs, sashaying toward the elevator. It was like watching life pass by in dreamy, Hollywood-style slow-mo, life with all its loveliness and messiness. And I smiled at it all.

I came to think of myself as the Airport Ambassador of Goodwill that day, perched on my chair, offering smiles like pieces of candy to the steady flow of travelers. I was astonished by how many people smiled back, sort of like we all somehow knew we were in it together, part of the big, soupy, stewy, messy, luscious mix of life. As I sat in that chair, smiling my Goodwill Ambassador smile, I realized one simple truth: all we could do, really, was be good to one another and care for one another. Because we were all in it together.

Later that evening—yes, I was *still* sitting in the airport as day crossed over to night—I eavesdropped on a woman talking on a cell phone to her family:

Hi, hon. Yeah, I'm still here...I think we're boarding soon, though. Yeah. Hey, I wanted to ask, did she take a shower tonight?... Yeah, she has bell choir in the morning... Oh, she's still up? Yeah, I'll talk to her. Hi, sweetie! Did you have a great day? Yeah? Wow! That does sound fun. Did I bring you presents? Yes, I brought you a little something... Okay, you have a good sleep, okay?... I'll be home late, but I'll come in and give you a kiss tonight.

I slumped down in the seat, tipped my chin toward my chest, closed my eyes, and settled into the warmth of my parka. As I listened to the comforting rhythm and soothing words of a conversation that felt like home, a conversation so familiar, so warm, it was like wrapping myself in a fleece bathrobe, I was struck again by the breadth of common experience, the universality of human life. That mother was no different from me, I realized. She was me talking to Noah and Rowan. She was every mom talking to every child.

I suspect I would have continued in this half trance, caught in the reverie of the moment, had I not been startled by a man behind me, who sneezed. Loudly. Three times in a row. The kind of sneeze that makes you wonder, *Really? Was that* really *necessary?* I glanced up to see another man seated across from me, an older, professorial type wearing a taupe trench coat. A dinged-up leather bag sat crumpled at his feet. As our gaze connected, his eyes crinkled in amusement and a subtle smirk turned up one corner of his mouth. Suddenly, without warning, we were both laughing, two strangers sitting at an airport gate, howling together until we finally got ahold of ourselves. And then, just as we settled down again, the professor leaned toward me and whispered, "Better take Airborne!" and we began again, laughing so hard we were nearly crying. Really, I had no idea why we were laughing. Maybe the professor, like me, had sucked down one too many Starbucks, but it was lovely—communal and friendly, two strangers connecting in a Minnesota airport.

"There is no way of telling people that they are all walking around shining like the sun," Thomas Merton once wrote.[4] For one brief moment, as I sat at the gate laughing and crying with my fellow travelers, I got it. We are all walking around shining like the sun. And it's all the result of God's grace. I had realized and appreciated the gift of seven precious hours because of God's grace. I had smiled at strangers because of God's grace. I had laughed along with the professor in the taupe trench coat because of God's grace. "This is beautiful, people. Are you getting it? Are you feeling it?" I wanted to shout as I looked at the world-weary travelers who sat around me. "Do you see it? Are you with me?" They weren't with me right at that moment; they didn't see as clearly as I did right then. But it really didn't matter.

That day in the airport I began to understand that belief in God encompasses something bigger, broader, deeper, and stronger than I'd realized, something that can't be neatly packaged and reasonably rationalized. Something I can't altogether explain; something that can include the highs—the glimpses of clarity, the moments of abundant life—as well as the lows—the questions and the pondering and the wrestling. Not only did I begin to understand a belief in God as altogether something more than I could ever fully define, contain, or pin down, I began to accept and embrace this understanding, in spite of the fact that it didn't fit well with my everything-has-a-place-and-an-order-and-a-rational-explanation expectations. As a result, I began to live more fully and freely in the "Why not?" I'd loosened another button on the stiff corset; I'd unclasped another buckle in the armor. A bright, steady shaft of light pierced the haze.

Bible Banger

> The Word became flesh and
> blood, and moved into the
> neighborhood.
> —JOHN 1:14, MSG

I didn't read the Bible as a kid. No one in my family did, as far as I could tell. My mom kept a thin King James Bible stashed in the back of her underwear drawer, and occasionally I'd slide it out, impressed by the gilded edges and the almost translucent onion-skin paper, mesmerized by the waterfall of gold that slipped through my fingers when I flipped the pages. But I never once saw her read it. Nor did I ever see a Bible in either of my grandparents' homes. They may have owned a Bible, but it certainly wasn't placed front and center on the coffee table or even on a bookshelf. My sister and I were given an illustrated children's Bible for Christmas, but we didn't read that either. It was shelved next to the Time Life science books on the dusty bookcase in the basement.

That's not to say I didn't know what the Bible was. I was familiar with it from a distance. I saw it float down the aisle of Saint Joseph's at the beginning and end of Mass every Saturday evening, held aloft by the acolyte, purple ribbons streaming. It looked weighty, grandiose, mysterious. I even heard passages read from it, the reader intoning from the pulpit and the congregation repeating the responsorial psalm. I knew about the Ten Commandments; I'd memorized them in catechism class before I made my First Communion. But I never considered that the Bible might be meant for me, personally, for my own eyes to see, fingers gliding over words on the page. I considered it sacred and venerated—a book for me to hear, perhaps, but not for me to read on my own.

As I watched the Bible with its fluttering ribbons and ornate cover float down the aisle each week, I understood my connection to God's Word. It was lofty, unattainable—literally held above my head, just out of reach.

During the season when I attended church fairly regularly (aside from my occasional jaunts to Barnes & Noble) but still remained on the fringe of belief, I decided I ought to look into this Jesus a bit more on my own. Clearly he played a prominent role with Lutherans, so I figured I'd better fill in some of the gaps. "So," I asked my husband one day, "is there such thing as a biography of Jesus?"

"Yeah," Brad answered, not missing a beat. "That would be the Bible."

I was sort of hoping for something more like *The Life and Times of*

Jesus Christ. I was pretty sure I knew the standard profile of a Bible-owning person, and I was pretty sure I didn't qualify. I certainly couldn't see myself spouting Scripture or engaging in a theological debate. I couldn't even see myself keeping a Bible on my bedside table. People who read the Bible were the kind of people who tagged their Halloween candy with Jesus messages and never had a glass of wine and went to church on Sundays *and* Wednesdays and sent their kids to Vacation Bible School, whatever that was. That person wasn't me. On the other hand, I *was* curious. Lutherans talked about the Bible an awful lot. Besides, I reasoned, it couldn't hurt to own one. I certainly didn't have to *display* it.

Making the actual purchase, though, challenged both my pride and my frail faith.

I walked into Barnes & Noble with a strategy. First I flipped through a few issues of *Dog Fancy* and *Poodle Review* to throw onlookers off my trail. Then I browsed the highly respectable New in Paperback table. And finally I moseyed over to the religion books, the sign blaring Christian Inspiration like a neon beacon above my head. Christian Inspiration was located conspicuously off the main aisle, right next to the information desk and across from the fiction stacks, where everyone could see who was browsing there and at what.

I felt self-conscious. Could the Bibles be in a more visible location? Did they do this intentionally as some sort of test of religious conviction? Were the floor plan gurus a bunch of fundamentalists, tickled by the thought of the rest of us sweating it out in the strategically positioned Christian Inspiration section?

As I glanced around sheepishly I began to plan my alibi in case I ran into, say, Kelli from work. "Oh my gosh. How totally bizarre!

How did I end up *here*? I was actually looking for *Origami 1-2-3*!"
Seriously, I think I would have rather had someone catch me leafing
through *The Pop-Up Book of Sex* than culling through the Christian
Inspiration section.

I thought buying a Bible would be a cinch. It's a Bible, right? How
complicated can one book be? Turns out, pretty complicated.

First of all, the shelves were labeled with mysterious acronyms:
NIV, NLT, KJV, GNT, RSV, NRSV. What did all the abbreviations mean? As
I crouched down to read the spines, I felt like I had wandered into the
military section—there were just so many acronyms. First there was
NIV, short for New International Version—perhaps the Gospels with a
bit of Asian flair? KJV, that was an easy one and the only version that
rang a bell, courtesy of my college Renaissance Literature days and the
Bible in the back of my mother's underwear drawer: the King James
Version. GNT: the Good News Translation—now we were getting
somewhere, perhaps a Bible with a positive spin? And RSV, come to
find out, did not refer to the respiratory virus but to Revised Standard
Version. As opposed, I assumed, to the once popular Standard Version. But here was my question…why would anyone buy the Revised
Standard Version if there was now an NRSV, a New Revised Standard
Version? Likewise, I saw NLT, which stood for New Living Translation,
but did this imply there was also an LT, a Living Translation? That
didn't seem to be the case.

Did there really need to be this many choices? I wondered. Weren't
they all saying basically the same thing? And where in the world was
BB, Basic Bible? That's all I was there for, a basic Bible. I couldn't even
figure out how to *buy* a Bible for heaven's sake. How in the world was
I actually going to *read* it?

I finally chose the *Life Application Bible: New International Version,* and frankly not for any good reason. I liked the title. That was me… applying Jesus to my life like a Band-Aid. And then, in bold yellow on the cover, there was the promotional note: "Today's #1 Selling Study Bible!" I've always been a sucker for advertising, so that got me. Plus I liked the word "study," which suggested I might find God through homework, a thought that appealed to my Type A, performance-driven self. Flipping through it, I also noticed the *Life Application Bible* was full of footnotes, and I am not kidding when I say footnotes are like comfort food for me. Any explanation of the cryptic, ancient text was a welcome addition. And finally, the real reason I chose the *Life Application Bible: New International Version* was that it simply felt right. It had hardcover heft but didn't scream "Bible banger" as some of the sumptuous leather-bound versions did.

When I finally made it to the register, I wouldn't look the cashier in the eye as I pushed the Bible across the counter. Self-conscious and embarrassed, I was worried she'd think I was a fundamentalist. "Would you like that in a sack?" she asked, and I nodded, busying myself with my wallet, grateful as she slipped the heavy book into the opaque plastic bag.

I didn't touch that Bible for a good long time. The process of purchasing it had rattled me so much I couldn't bear to open the cover. Finally, too intimidated to delve into it on my own, I decided to sign up for a class at my church. "Introduction to Lutheranism" sounded innocuous enough.

The first night the ten of us met, Pastor Sara suggested we go around the table to introduce ourselves and tell one another what we hoped to gain from the class. I panicked. I'd sort of been hoping to slump in my chair and not say much for most of the class sessions. Certainly I didn't expect to face my age-old faith question on the very first night. What in the world was I going to say? "Hi, I'm Michelle. I've attended Southwood Lutheran for five years on and off...that is, when I'm not visiting the Barnes & Noble magazine section to bone up on whether Angelina Jolie is 'scary skinny' or just regular skinny this week. I, well, maybe...probably, well...I'm not sure but sometimes I think I do but sometimes I think I don't believe in God. I hope to find Jesus in this class." I might as well throw myself out there like a wriggling worm for the churchies to snap me up in one bite.

So instead, I hedged, just as I'd always done when I faced any question related to faith. "Hi, I'm Michelle," I said, looking down at my lap. "I've been a member of Southwood for five years [throat clear]. And I hope to broaden my faith more by attending this class." Yeah. And that was about as close to the truth as Bill Clinton's "I did not have sexual relations with that woman" proclamation.

A survey of my classmates that night practically had me breathing into a paper bag. Ray was raised Missouri Synod (read: pseudo-Catholic). Katharine had been a practicing Lutheran all her life, praise Jesus. Beatrice and Arnold—weren't they sweet with their Bibles zipped into matching maroon cases?—had been Southwood members for twenty-six years. Oh, and then there was the former Pentecostal, George. I made a mental note to sit far, far away from George in case he decided to start speaking in tongues. And so on. As far as I could tell, I was the only person in the room who was not a dyed-in-the-wool believer. Once again, I was way out of my element. The woman who still wasn't 100 percent sure she believed in God was sitting in a Bible study class.

With the frightening introductions complete, Pastor Sara asked us to turn to Exodus. I flipped nervously through the thin pages of my brand-new Bible. Okay, there was Deuteronomy, Samuel, Esther— who the heck was Esther?—Psalms, Matthew, Mark, Acts, Revelation… Where was Exodus? I actually wondered for a second if I'd purchased a translation without Exodus. Maybe I had missed the fine print: "NIV, ME—New International Version, Minus Exodus." I frantically flipped back and forth until finally Beatrice leaned over and whispered kindly, "Dear, it's a little more toward the front." Perfect. I wasn't even in the right Testament.

Despite my initial urge to run screaming from the room that night, I went back for the second class, and again and again, enrolling in more Bible study and religious adult education classes: "How to Pray"—I needed this one big time—"Lutheranism in America," "The Psalms." I even, gasp, began reading the Bible at night before bed. It made a great sleep tonic; a few pages of Matthew or Luke and I was zonked.

Then I took on the big guns, enrolling in a twelve-week New Testament class that met once a week for the entire summer. This gang was different. We weren't talking church elders with their Sunday morning bowties and rouged cheeks, trying to extend the weekend socializing just a bit more before heading home for the Swanson turkey and gravy and *Wheel of Fortune.* These people were serious, middle-aged professionals; these people were *studying* the Bible. My only hope was that perhaps my slight literary edge would carry me through. After plunking down eighty-nine dollars (I admit, I shuddered at the thought of the shoes I could buy with that eighty-nine dollars) for our companion text, *New Testament Story: An Introduction,* I dove in and realized to my delight that the author employed a literary approach, exploring the nuances of language and tossing forth words like *hermeneutical* and *rhetoric* with ease. *Oh yeah, come to mama,* I thought, flipping through the first assignment. I'd been an English major, after all. As I read the text before the first class, I felt like I'd come home.

"Man," I bragged to Brad, "my classmates are seriously not going to know what hit them reading this literary stuff. I'm not worried at all. I'm going to be just fine." I felt confident, in control, and in my element as I pictured myself explaining the concepts of various literary devices to my Biblemates the next night.

That's not exactly how it went.

I quickly discovered that my classmates were educated, well-read, and, well, wicked smart. These people actually knew what they were talking about; in fact, they spoke with confidence, experience, and authority. *Allegory* was clearly a familiar term; *rhetoric* didn't ruffle them a bit. One guy even pronounced *hermeneutics* correctly, for Pete's sake. Suddenly it all became shockingly clear: *I* was the only one in over my head. Sitting in class on the first night, I silently freaked out, my confidence oozing out of me like a gas leak. I felt intimidated, stupid, and worst of all, fake. It seemed everyone else was there for the right reasons—for example, to grow their relationship with Jesus—while I was *pretending* to be there for the right reasons. I was worried I'd be exposed as a Christian fraud, a spiritual joke, an impostor. Before too long, they would realize I was most definitely not one of them.

So I made a radical decision: I decided right then and there that blunt honesty was my best bet. I was sick of pretending anyway, tired of wearing the mask of the model God-loving and God-fearing Christian. I decided to admit once and for all that I didn't know what I was doing, what I thought, what I believed, even sometimes *if* I truly believed. I would tell the truth: I wasn't like them; I didn't fit in. I wasn't a proper Christian. I didn't have it all together like they did. Why not, I figured? What in the world did I have to lose?

My classmates adjusted to the authentic me pretty well. As time went on that summer, I think I was viewed with affectionate wariness as the black sheep of the group. But that was okay. It was such a relief to be myself, waffling warts, blurty doubts, spiritual awkwardness, and all. Occasionally my responses were met with uncomfortable silence, like the time I suggested Paul was a pompous egomaniac with an insecurity complex. (One woman retorted dryly that Paul must have done something right, given that there is a church on every corner named after him.) But sometimes my questions prompted lively discussion. And every now and then the other group members opened up as well, including the physician's assistant who tentatively admitted he was seeking, and not finding, miracles in the present day. And the lawyer who seemed befuddled by seeming inconsistencies in the Gospels.

Then there was Maryann. The most conservative member of the group, Maryann made me nervous. I could barely make eye contact with her, half-afraid she harbored some kind of Christ power that could send me careening to hell the second I voiced my doubts. But it was a small class, and she was a vocal member. There was no hiding from Maryann.

Maryann made frequent mention of what she called the Left Behind books. At first I assumed she was referring to writings that didn't make it into the final version of the Bible. But as it turned out, she was a fan of the series by Tim LaHaye and Jerry B. Jenkins that fictionalizes the end times prophesied in the books of Revelation, Isaiah, and

Ezekiel. I knew all this about Maryann preceding our discussion of Revelation, so her take on the Second Coming shouldn't have come as a surprise. But it did.

Now let me be clear here: I'm the first to admit that I will have to read Revelation another fifty-six times to digest even an iota of what it's all about. Maryann, on the other hand, had it figured out. "I am ready, right now, to witness Jesus ride in on his white horse," she announced without warning one night. "I'm serious," she added, in case we doubted her. "Right now, right here in this classroom, I'm ready. I want to be right there when he appears in his robe dipped in blood and rides in with his sword in his mouth and takes down all those who have rejected him. I'm ready to stand back and watch that. I want to see who is left standing."

Call me paranoid, but I swear Maryann looked straight at me.

There was an awkward pause, a moment of silence in the classroom before I blurted, "Whoa, whoa there! Okay now, no need to rush things. Let's just slow down a bit here. I need more time. I'm *so* not ready to see the white horse!"

I wasn't mocking Maryann that night, and I'm still not. Maryann was like my mom (well, a slightly more radical version of my mom). She believed 100 percent, no questions asked. And that was far more appealing than my particular brand of irresolute faith. I wanted Maryann's confidence and yearned for her enthusiasm. I was envious of her rock-solid faith, her true belief. I wanted to be a Christian insider like Maryann, someone who had it all together and had her faith ducks lined up in a perfect row.

Above all, Maryann's declarations uncovered a deep fear in me. I worried that I questioned and doubted too much and that my tenuous steps toward faith would never culminate in Maryann's kind of confidence. I fretted that my "Why not?" seemed flimsy and pathetic compared to Maryann's bold, swaggering faith, like a spindly, leggy petunia next to the *helianthus giganteus* (otherwise known as the mammoth sunflower). Frankly, I even worried about the fact that I was so worried. Worrying about the strength of my faith—how it stood up to others'—didn't seem to be a healthy sign. I mean, didn't worrying about faith defeat the whole point of faith? Weren't we supposed to just "let go and let God"? I didn't "let go and let God" very well. I worried about that.

Truthfully, reading the Bible didn't often assuage my worry. In fact, sometimes it even fueled it. Cracking open the Bible and jumping in feet first was tough. I was lucky I had the New Testament class, scary Maryann and all, to guide me. But even with that structure in place, I struggled. It didn't take long, once I started reading the Bible, to figure out that Jesus's teachings were tough to live by.

I fretted over passages such as the parable in Matthew about the wedding feast, a story that seemed to me a little unfair. In the parable a king hosts a wedding banquet for his son. The people he invites to the festivities don't show up, so he orders his servants out to the street corners to invite anyone they can find to the reception. Within minutes the banquet hall is teeming with guests who have happily lined up for a bit of "fattened cattle," spirits, and a good time. It's a motley crew at best, including a man dressed inappropriately for a wedding. No surprise there, given the situation, yet for some reason this angers the king, who demands to know, "How did you get in here without wedding clothes?" The guest's reaction is one of the best lines in the story: "The man was speechless." Of course he's speechless; he's thinking,

You dope, your people dragged me in off the street and now you expect me to be wearing a tux? He can't say what he's thinking to the king, of course, so instead he's tied "hand and foot" and thrown outside into the darkness, where there is "weeping and gnashing of teeth." The parable concludes with this statement, uttered by the king: "For many are invited, but few are chosen" (Matthew 22:1–14).

I read this passage countless times and pored over the footnotes, and still it baffled me. I didn't get it. Obviously I knew the king represented Jesus, and the original invitees were the religious people who ultimately rejected Jesus and his teaching. That part I understood. But what didn't resonate with me one bit was the poor beggar guy. He thought he'd been invited, he'd settled comfortably into his role as a wedding guest, but before he could dust off his trousers and tuck in his shirt, he was thrown out of the hall and deemed unchosen.

So this was what worried me: Who was to say *I* wasn't the beggar guy? It seemed like I was invited; I was working pretty hard to join the faith feast, but who was to say that in the end I wouldn't tumble into darkness for an eternity of teeth gnashing in the stinky sulfur lake? What if I had been invited, but I had not been *chosen*? According to the Bible, there was a big gap between being invited and being chosen.

Contrary to the feel-good message I often heard at my new church, I found the Gospels weren't brimming only with love and grace. They also included some tough language and strict orders. I naturally gravitated toward the passages that made sense and those that sounded peaceful and loving. It was tempting to pick through the Bible and embrace what was easy or logical or sounded good on paper, while rejecting the tough stuff, the stuff that challenged, frightened, or seemed downright implausible. Walking on water seemed outlandish; a virgin birth, incomprehensible; feeding thousands with a mere handful of loaves and fishes, crazy. Jesus was too harsh here, too critical there, and the Holy Spirit—who in the world could make sense of him…or it…or whatever it was? A quote often attributed to Augustine points out the flaw in my approach: "If you believe what you like in the Gospels, and reject what you don't like, it is not the Gospels you believe, but yourself." By the time I was done analyzing, theorizing, rationalizing, mulling, doubting, and questioning, not much remained that I could easily embrace.

Luther observed that those of us who analyze the Bible and use reason to interpret it aren't actually hearing God's Word but instead are trying to master it, control it, manipulate it, and make it our own. Rational, analytical person that I am, I dissected the Bible, deconstructing Jesus's words and lessons, discarding those I deemed out of date or inappropriate or just plain weird while embracing the ones that worked, the ones that I could understand and achieve. This approach, Luther warned, would get me nowhere.

"But if you insist that you be heard, that your reason interpret Christ's word; if you presume to play the master of the word, to propound other doctrines, if you probe it, measure it, and twist the words to read as you want them to, brood over them, hesitate, doubt, and then judge them according to your reason—that is not hearing the word or being its pupil," said Luther in one of his *Sermons on the Gospel of St. John*. In dissecting the Bible this way you establish yourself as the teacher, rather than the follower, and in doing so, Luther warned, "you will never discover the meaning of Christ's word or of his heavenly

Father's will."[1] The more I read the Bible, the more I realized that in nitpicking I lost the big picture, and, more important, I missed the whole point.

As I forged my way through the Bible for the first time, Rowan decided he wanted to give it a try too. So every night before bed we read a bit from the Old Testament in the children's Bible he had received as a gift. Rowan was transfixed by the stories. Some nights he even chose the Bible over Harry Potter (why I gave him the choice of the Bible or Harry Potter is another question entirely). The trouble was, you can't read the Bible, especially the Old Testament, without stumbling into 146 tricky questions. So every night Rowan and I delved into Theology 101.

He was particularly troubled by the story of the mothers in 1 Kings 3. "Why would the king cut the baby in half?" he asked, eyes wide, brow furrowed. I explained the concept again and again: that King Solomon wasn't really going to take his sword and cut a living baby in two. He was merely trying to trick the truth out of the two women in order to discern who was the real mother. The morning after our reading and discussion, though, I heard Rowan ask Brad the question again as he hunched over his bowl of Rice Krispies. Clearly he remembered who had the theology degree in the house.

The story of Abraham and Isaac also posed some problems. "Would you kill me if God told you to?" Rowan asked, interrupting me just as Abraham raised the knife over his son.

I hesitated. "No," I admitted as we snuggled beneath the comforter. "Abraham was very brave and had a lot of faith in God to trust that his son wouldn't be harmed. But I think I might be too afraid to have that much trust in God." He seemed relieved by my answer, even when I reminded him that God wasn't the kind of God who would really make me kill my own son.

"Why is God so mean?" Rowan asked in the middle of some stories, such as when we read the book of Job. "Why is God so mad?" he inquired when we read of the Israelites wandering in the wilderness and their exile in Babylon.

I tried to explain. "In the old, old days, before Jesus, people used to give God animals as a way to thank him and honor him," I told Rowan. "But they kept disobeying God and forgetting about him. And that made God mad and sad." I told Rowan that later God sent us his son, Jesus, and Jesus became all the animals wrapped into one gift when he died on the cross, which is why we don't have to give God animals anymore. I didn't mention the bloody parts—the animal sacrifices and the burnt offerings. But then we read 1 Kings 18, the story where Elijah's sacrifice to God proved more powerful than King Ahab's sacrifice to the false god Baal, and I was forced to explain the history of sacrifice to Rowan. The fact was, I couldn't simply avoid the unsavory parts of the Bible, even in a children's version.

Reading the Old Testament taught Rowan and me some hard truths about sin. But it also illustrated why Jesus was such a necessary and bright light in our lives. "We need Jesus," I reminded Rowan. "We can't obey God all on our own; it's too hard. We make too many mistakes." Rowan nodded, seeming to understand. Still, I was relieved when we completed the Old Testament readings. With Matthew on deck for the following night, I was ready to welcome Jesus and the New Testament. The funny thing was, Rowan tired of the New Testament; it didn't hold his attention nearly as well. "I miss the stories," he admitted a few nights later, as we read the Sermon on the Mount. Like me, Rowan was inclined to focus on his favorite parts of the Bible, too, and neglect the verses that didn't appeal to him as much.

Reading Rowan's simplified children's Bible also helped illuminate one very important detail I hadn't previously noticed. God often seemed to choose the least likely candidate for the job. He chose flawed people, doubting people, sinful people. He chose the misfits. In particular, the story of Jacob stood out to me. Jacob, it turned out, was a wrestler, just like me.

As the story unfolds in Genesis 32, a man approaches Jacob when he is unprotected and vulnerable, alone on the riverbank in the middle of the night. The two wrestle, and their battle is a long one, waged through the entire night until dawn breaks. Then this exchange takes place:

> When the man saw that he could not overpower him, he
> touched the socket of Jacob's hip so that his hip was wrenched
> as he wrestled with the man. Then the man said, "Let me go,
> for it is daybreak."
>
> But Jacob replied, "I will not let you go unless you bless
> me."
>
> The man asked him, "What is your name?"
>
> "Jacob," he answered.
>
> Then the man said, "Your name will no longer be Jacob,
> but Israel, because you have struggled with God and with
> humans and have overcome." (verses 25–28)

I immediately noticed the word *wrestle* in these verses. The text didn't read "argue" or even "fight," but instead used the highly charged verb "wrestle," a very specific word choice evoking very particular images—images of grown men rolling around on the ground, grunting, struggling, entangled; of bulging muscles and sweaty bodies; of competition, power, and violence. This interaction between God and Jacob was clearly not a discussion, or even a heated argument. It was a battle, a physical match.

To me, this story seemed less about the struggle itself and more about the simple fact that God allows us to wrestle with him. I understood that God condones wrestling, even encourages it, because struggle is a catalyst for transformation. God could have easily won the match with Jacob. In fact, when I looked closely at the passage, I noticed that in the end, when the time was right, God clearly did overpower his rival; he merely brushed Jacob's hip with his hand and left the man with a lasting injury. But God saw that Jacob needed the struggle in order to shed his old self and his old ways and grow closer in a genuine relationship with him. Wrestling with God enabled Jacob to trust God in his heart, on his own accord. God, it seemed, would not overpower my free will and *force* me to trust him. He wouldn't coerce genuine trust and love out of me; instead he would work through the process with me. Even if that process required a long and wearisome wrestling match.

The more I read of the Bible, the more apparent it became: God chose flawed people. Jacob, a wreck of a person—deceitful, selfish, and cunning—was encouraged to wrestle with God in order to persevere as the father of God's chosen people, the father of all nations. David, a murderer and adulterer, was chosen to carry on the ancestral line of Jesus. Peter, the man who wavered in his faith as he walked across the water and later betrayed Jesus not once but three times, was chosen as the rock, the one who would spread the good news and help build the early Christian church. Many of the people I met in the Bible, including the disciples themselves, turned out to be ordinary humans—flawed, fallible, and struggling. Yet through these ordinary people and despite their many imperfections, God accomplished great things.

This realization gave me hope, hope that my questions and doubts and wrestling and waffling were all an important part of my journey, part of the growing pains I would experience in my deepening relationship with God. Peter told me I could waver. David told me I didn't need to be perfect. Jacob told me it was okay to wrestle. And through these people and their stories, God told me he chose me again and again. In spite of my flaws.

One Sunday I sat in the pew and watched as the third-graders in our congregation stood at the altar to be presented with Bibles. I was struck by one important detail: the pastor presided over the brief ceremony, but the parents themselves, not the pastor, handed the Bibles to their children. The Word of God was handed, literally and figuratively, from parent to child.

How different from my own experience, I thought, as I clapped with the rest of the congregation while the kids filed proudly back to the pews, new Bibles tucked beneath their arms. It had taken thirty-five years for me to own my own Bible; thirty-five years for the Bible to be transformed from untouchable to touched, from not-for-me to mine. In that moment I realized that my Bible had become a tool. Sacred, yes; holy, yes; but also read, paged-through, dog-eared, underlined, and studied, rather than merely revered from a distance. God's Word—and Jesus himself—had moved into my neighborhood and into my life.

"Faith comes from hearing the message," said Paul in Romans 10:17. "And the message is heard through the word about Christ." As long as I kept my tool handy, as long as I kept the Bible in front of me, its heft in my hands, its pages between my fingers, rather than relegating it to a dusty top shelf, I continued to hear the message that God loves me and accepts me exactly as I am. C. S. Lewis emphasized the necessity of Bible study this way:

> If you want to get any further, you must use the map.... A vague religion—all about feeling God in nature, and so on— is so attractive. It is all thrills and no work; like watching the waves from the beach. But you will not get to Newfoundland by studying the Atlantic that way, and you will not get eternal life by simply feeling the presence of God in flowers or music. Neither will you get anywhere by looking at maps without going to sea. Nor will you be very safe if you go to sea without a map.[2]

I had gone to sea. Sometimes I was swept out to the murky, chilly depths on a swift and violent riptide. Sometimes I would tread frantically, my head barely above the water. Sometimes I splashed with carefree abandon. But always, always I had the map in the midst of the sea of faith.

It was not an ordinary map; it didn't have a grid of highways and interstates all pointing in the right direction, and it often sent me on the more circuitous scenic route. There weren't any shortcuts on my map either, no Panama Canal to abbreviate a great and laborious distance. Occasionally I tossed it aside, frustrated by its twisting routes and lack of clear signage. But I always picked up the map once more, shook off the water droplets, and began to follow the route again. The map was my guide, my lifeboat, my beacon.

I had gone to sea and had taken my map, swimming my way to a newfound land.

Shedding the One-Size-Fits-All Faith

> Christian conversion is, in fact,
> incarnational; it is worked out
> by each individual within the
> community of faith.
> —KATHLEEN NORRIS

My conversation with Pastor Greg had given me hope that doubt and faith could coexist. The problem was, my brand-new shaky faith was still as fragile as a Fabergé egg.

For a long time after that pastoral encounter, and even after I'd felt the warming of my heart, I was afraid to tell a soul. I was terrified that my new faith was fake; ironically, I didn't have faith in my faith. It was sort of like buying a new pair of shoes. Often, especially if they are on the pricey side, I'll bring my new shoes home and stash the box in my closet, slipping on the sling-backs or platforms in the evening to wear inside the house. But until I'm sure those shoes fit, that they don't rub my heel raw or pinch my toes, I don't wear them outside, because I know I can't return them once the soles get scuffed.

My new faith was a bit like that. I would take it out in secret, examine how it felt, try to determine if it was a good fit. But then I would shove it back in the box, pull the lid over it, and slip it into the back of my closet, unwilling to go public until I was sure I'd decided to keep it.

Kathleen Norris said this about the "no faith in faith" predicament in *Amazing Grace:* "When seeking the holy becomes a goal in itself, the last thing we want to do is *find* it.... Anything that feels like finding translates into commitment. And like conversion itself, commitment is scary."[1]

I had a problem with commitment. I was afraid to proclaim that I had found Jesus, been saved, boarded the boat bound for eternal life. I figured it wasn't something I could announce one week and then a month or two later admit, "Oh yeah, sorry, people. That was my Jesus phase. I'm into transcendental meditation now." I wanted to be sure. Well, as sure as I could possibly be...which, it turns out, is not very sure.

One issue that stymied me was that I still wanted proof. Even after I experienced my warm-heart moment and began the slow inching back toward faith, I still yearned for cold, hard proof of God's existence. And I wanted proof that faith worked too.

I was particularly disappointed in a research study that analyzed the effects of prayer on the recovery of more than eighteen hundred heart patients over a ten-year period. Results of the study had been eagerly anticipated by both the medical and faith communities alike, and as I read through a report on the findings, I was intrigued, on one hand gravely skeptical, on the other hand hopeful that I would finally be offered the hard-core proof I desired.

The results of the scientific study unequivocally concluded that prayers offered by strangers had absolutely no effect on the physical recovery of the heart surgery patients. Some evidence even suggested that those patients who knew they were being prayed for fared *worse* than those who did not know they were being prayed for. Researchers surmised that awareness of the fact that strangers were praying for them may have caused performance anxiety in some of the patients. "It may have made them uncertain, wondering am I so sick they had to call in their prayer team?" concluded cardiologist Dr. Charles Bethea, a coauthor of the study, published in the *American Heart Journal.*[2]

This conclusion was definitely not the resounding proof of God I was looking for, and the explanation offered by Bob Barth, spiritual director for one of the churches that did the praying in the study, seemed flimsy next to the scientific evidence. "A person of faith would say that this study is interesting," said Barth in a *New York Times* article, "but we've been praying a long time and we've seen prayer work, we know it works."[3]

Wake up, Bob, the game's over, I thought bitterly when I read that. I couldn't dismiss the hard evidence presented by the study. After all this was *science,* and in my mind science still trumped all. Science was definitive; there was no wiggle room. If sound scientific analysis found prayer didn't work, then it didn't work, case closed. And if prayer didn't work, might the next logical conclusion be that God didn't exist? I still couldn't quite extinguish that niggling question, that doubt, from my mind.

As time passed, I also continued to wrestle with the fact that my faith felt like more of a head thing than a heart thing. It seemed as if I had an intellectual faith rather than an emotional faith, like I knew God in my head but not deep in my heart. It felt a little bit like how I'd approached high school chemistry, when I memorized all the individual elements on the periodic table but didn't have a clue how they worked together.

One day I sat in church and listened to a fellow member talk about her call to do mission work at Southwood's sister church in La Ceibita, Honduras. She spoke passionately about the actual moment she'd felt her calling. She had been sitting in the pew on a regular old Sunday, just as I was on that day, listening to another member speak about a mission trip, when suddenly she felt an overwhelming, nearly physical force sweep through her body. She knew with absolute conviction that she was being called to South America. The woman's eyes welled, her voice grew raspy, and she fought to rein in her emotion as she stood at the pulpit and described her experience. She was genuine, and she wore her love and fervor for Jesus front and center on her sleeve.

But throughout her compelling talk, I could think only one thing: *I don't feel like that. Why don't I feel that way about Jesus? Why am I not getting all worked up and emotional over my faith?* I worried my faith wasn't deep or strong enough. I wondered if my lack of emotion was an indication that my faith wasn't authentic. I wondered if this woman and all real believers had tapped into something I was missing.

In his book *Blue Like Jazz,* Donald Miller suggests that loving Jesus is something you feel, something that may be hard to pin down, difficult to get down on paper, but "no less real, no less meaningful, no less beautiful."[4] I think this was what the missionary woman experienced when she tried to convey the depth of her passion—an overwhelming impression of bigness, a sensation surging from her heart rather than a conscious thought processed in her brain. As she stood at the pulpit fighting tears, I saw that she struggled to translate into language the magnitude of what she felt for God in her heart. But while words proved inadequate, her response was not. She took that surge in her heart, and she translated it into action, dedicating her life to mission work in Honduras and sharing the story of her calling with others.

After I heard that woman speak in church, I began to ask myself some hard questions. "Do you feel it, really *feel* it?" I asked. "Do you feel love for God and faith in your heart? Do you have an overwhelming, overpowering, genuine love for God? Do you feel that same love surging toward you, from God?" More often than not, the answer was no. I couldn't imagine myself ever crying over my love for Jesus. I couldn't even imagine myself working Jesus into an everyday conversation with neighbors or friends. Although I'd opened the door to belief and stepped through, I still didn't feel like I fit the part. I had in my head a picture of the ideal Christian—perhaps something a little Hollywoodish, the image of a newly converted believer rising from the baptismal waters—and because I wasn't emotionally on fire for Jesus, because my faith didn't seem to align with that idealized picture, it seemed as if I fell short.

I'll never forget the first time I read the story in Luke 7 about the woman who interrupted Jesus's dinner with the Pharisees to pour perfume on his feet and wipe them clean with her hair. I was immediately uncomfortable with this woman, not because she was a sinner, a "bad person," an "immoral woman," but because of the way she loved Jesus.

Part of me wanted to tell the foot-kissing, hair-wiping, weeping woman to get ahold of herself, to get up off the floor, stop making a scene, and act properly. Her dramatic display of adoration and affection made me uneasy. It made me uncomfortable because it was so raw, such a pure, extravagant, over-the-top display. But part of me was envious of her wholehearted, emphatic love. Part of me wanted to know what it felt like to love Jesus that way.

As I read the story I tried to envision how I would react if I met Jesus in person. I imagined I might offer him a cup of tea, maybe shake his hand, stammer that I admire his work. But would I throw myself at his feet? Would I weep for joy? Would I pour my whole self into the moment, toss caution to the wind, disregard what anyone might think or say about me and simply love him with abandon?

I doubt it.

Intellectually I knew that God loved me. And I knew I was supposed to love God. But I didn't *feel* the kind of love the missionary woman had articulated during her testimony, the kind of love the woman with the alabaster perfume jar seemed to feel when she wept at Jesus's feet. It seemed I was missing the emotional link, the connection that made that kind of love possible. I couldn't see myself loving Jesus with my head *and* my heart. On most days the head alone was hard enough. And so I began to wonder if faith, that kind of love for and belief in God, was an innate sort of conviction, something a person was born with. Was faith something a person either had or didn't have? And if so, where did that leave someone like me, someone lacking such heart-based, emotional conviction? Was I doomed?

When I found myself disheartened by my lack of an emotionally charged faith, I figured I had two choices. I could obsess over why I didn't feel a connection to God in my heart and why I was never moved to tears by my love for Jesus, or I could simply continue to put one foot in front of the other. I could try to figure out the next step in my faith journey and move forward.

As I slowly grew more connected to my church community, I observed that many of Southwood's members seemed passionate about serving, both locally in Lincoln and abroad. I noticed the dozens of individuals and families who traveled thousands of miles on their own dime to build houses and minister to the people at our sister churches in Tanzania and Honduras. I took note of the members who mentored adolescents in need of positive role models, the volunteers who served every week at the free health clinic downtown, and even the man who single-handedly baked 120 dozen doughnut holes each and every Sunday to be served at Southwood's café.

I was especially moved by the story of retired Lutheran pastor Harold Hamilton. I first heard about Harold when Pastor Greg mentioned him in a sermon, and I learned more about him from an article in the local paper. This was a man in his late eighties who had already dedicated several decades of his professional life ministering to the people of Lincoln, a man who in his role as a pastor had visited hundreds of sick and dying patients, mourned with hundreds of grieving families, soothed hundreds of world-weary congregants, guided hundreds of lost souls, and preached thousands of inspirational words. This was a person who could have said, in good conscience, "I deserve a rest. I'm entitled to a break." Yet what did Harold do? He continued to serve.

Harold pored over the grocery flyers every Sunday to scope out the best deals and then spent most weekday mornings plodding from store to store, purchasing items in bulk—cream of mushroom soup, Chex cereal, Rice-A-Roni, whatever was on sale—and delivering the food to local charities around town. His basement looked like a stockroom. His garage was piled floor to ceiling with food. He served humbly, without fanfare and with little acknowledgment. Harold didn't feel the need to announce his good deeds to the world. He didn't need a clap on the back; he didn't need to boast about his generosity or sacrifice. He simply and quietly served.

Compare all that to what I might have done in Harold's shoes. For starters, I would have kicked back the recliner, flipped on *Antiques Roadshow,* and had myself a good snooze. I might have met my friends for coffee and pecan rolls Tuesday mornings at Village Inn. Perhaps I would have tried my hand at Sudoku. I can tell you with utmost certainty that I would not have spent my leisure time and my limited financial resources grocery shopping for the poor. I would not have dipped into my meager savings to stock the shelves of the food bank. If I had been in Harold's shoes, I would have assumed I'd already "done my part," completed my duty, and crossed off the final item on my Christian good deeds checklist. I would have patted myself on the back, felt pretty darn good about my contributions, and enjoyed a well-deserved rest.

Yet Harold's commitment and dedication inspired me. I didn't know him, and I certainly didn't know if he cried over his love for Jesus, but I could see from how he spent his time that Harold was a take-action kind of guy. He and the other believers I saw who put their faith into action outside the church walls reminded me that we are never done growing and living out our faith and, more important, that we are never done serving God and his people. To me, Harold's commitment to serving his community suggested that a pragmatic approach to faith was possible and even perhaps necessary.

One day I noticed in the church bulletin that a local faith-based educational program was looking for reading tutors to volunteer at a low-income elementary school in Lincoln. I e-mailed the program director and registered not only myself, but Brad too, volunteering us each for one short session a week at the reading center.

Signing up felt great; we both were excited and committed. But I'll be honest. Tutoring a fidgety second-grader at the end of a long day while he picked his nose, fell off his chair twice in ten minutes, and read with about as much emotional expression as Winston Churchill was not glamorous work. I had to resist glancing at my watch every 3.5 seconds, despite the fact that each session lasted less than forty minutes. Plus, as Samuel, my student, asked for the third time in ten minutes if we could play I Spy, I questioned why I was tutoring someone else's child, while one of my kids had his own homework to do and spelling list to practice. *Shouldn't I be making dinner or folding laundry or balancing my checkbook?* I wondered.

Then one evening the local news station aired a story about the success of the program, and the very next day, as I sat with Samuel at our table, a boy skipped across the classroom, twirling and trumpeting, "I told our story on TV! I told our story on TV!" It was Darveon, the fifth-grader who'd been interviewed for the news story. And in that jubilant skip, in those proud, ecstatic words, I heard the answers to my questions. Why was I sitting with Samuel during those forty minutes each week? Because of this: joy, pride, success, possibility, connection, promise, and hope.

It didn't matter that Samuel himself didn't articulate that glee. When I felt joy surge in my heart, the message was clear: This wasn't about me. It wasn't about proving to myself that my faith made a difference. And it wasn't solely about Samuel either. Those forty minutes Samuel and I spent together weren't about what either of us gained individually from the experience—how many words he read or how many minutes of my time I sacrificed or how deep my faith was. It was about relationship, human connection, and love.

Because I am by nature a concrete person, putting my faith into action in my greater community grew my faith in ways that sitting in church could not. I may never be an emotional, heart-on-my-sleeve kind of believer, but service to and with my community is a way for me to express and experience God's love in a concrete, tangible way.

After we'd been volunteering as reading tutors for a while, Brad and I decided it would be good for us to do some community service as a family. We settled on delivering Meals on Wheels. Every six weeks or so we drove to the food distribution center and loaded the heavy case of fifteen hot entrées and the plastic cooler of fifteen paper lunch bags into the minivan. Then, with maps spread out on the dashboard and the CD jangling, we set off.

Len in apartment 31 was always ready for us, sitting in his wheelchair at the table when we walked in the door—knife, fork, spoon, and plate arranged neatly on a place mat in front of him, a paper napkin tucked under his chin. He gratefully accepted Rowan's drawing and pointed at paintings on the walls and stacked on the floor. "I'm a portrait artist," he told the boys, and we admired the oil painting of a bullfighter with a golden costume and a scarlet cloth.

One floor up, Norma gave the boys a tour of her apartment. We chatted about her grandchildren and great-grandchildren. Noah admired the wreath of plastic autumn leaves hanging on her front door. "Thank you for taking the time to talk," she told us, closing the door quietly as we walked toward the elevator.

Ethel always asked Rowan if he had signed his name to the picture he drew for her. When he shook his head no, she would laugh and tell him she would remember who drew it anyway. "How could I forget the boy with that red, red hair?" she teased him.

One Saturday Noah slouched in the backseat of the minivan as we drove toward the next apartment, vocally unhappy about the pungent odor of cooked broccoli wafting from the back. When he complained of feeling gaggy, I rolled down all the windows so the damp, cold air would diminish the stench. Then I cranked the heat full blast to counter the Nebraska chill and passed back the box of Tic Tacs. "Here," I told him. "Suck on a Tic Tac. Maybe the mint will help."

Noah popped one into his mouth and then pressed another beneath his nose. He kept the Tic Tac under his nose for the entire two hours it took to complete our route.

"Why are we doing this?" he whined.

"We're doing this because it's God's work," I lectured through clenched teeth. "We're doing this because God loves when we help other people. Didn't you see how happy Norma was to show you the pictures of her grandkids? Didn't you see how excited Ethel was about Rowan's drawing?"

We pulled into the next driveway. When we rang Bev's doorbell,

I saw the light bulb flicker on and off, on and off, but she didn't answer. Bev was deaf, so her doorbell was rigged to a lamp in her living room that flashed to alert her when someone was at the door. I rang and rang, peering through the rectangular glass pane of her front door. I could see her slumped in her easy chair, chin to chest, a rumpled afghan slung across her shoulders. She was asleep. At least I hoped she was asleep. A TV tray piled high with pill bottles, Kleenex, and magazines was balanced at her side. Her oxygen tank was propped against the chair, and the television was on. I rang the bell five or six times, but Bev still didn't stir. "We'll have to come back after we finish our route," I announced to the boys as we climbed back into the van. "Maybe she'll be awake in twenty minutes."

"What! Come back?" Noah bellowed. "No! I don't want to come all the way back. I want to be done. I want to go home!"

I slammed the van into park and craned around to face him in the backseat. "Listen," I snapped. "Bev has no one. Why do you think she gets meals delivered on Saturday? Do you think she would get meals delivered if she had someone to cook her lunch and dinner like you do?"

Noah was quiet. "It just smells yucky in here," he said. "And I'm tired."

"I know, honey. I know," I answered. "I'm tired too. But sometimes we have to suffer a little bit to help people who suffer a lot."

We carried on that way for several months—the boys complaining and gagging, me lecturing and sighing from the driver's seat. One Saturday Brad brilliantly suggested smearing Vicks VapoRub beneath Noah's nose before we left the house, and that worked for a few weeks.

But the day I caught Noah's face in the rearview mirror, the VapoRub container clamped around his nose like a feedbag and his eyes swimming with tears, was the day we quit Meals on Wheels.

On one hand I felt like a failure for having initiated a project we couldn't complete. I'd seen other families pull up in their minivans outside the food distribution center. *Their* kids seemed to tolerate the wafting odor of broccoli just fine. Why were *my* kids the only ones who couldn't hack it? Why was *my* family the only family who'd flunked community service? *Maybe I shouldn't have given in so easily?* I wondered. *Maybe other parents, better Christian parents, real Christians, would have found a way to make it work.*

I was tempted to give up on family community service altogether. My kids clearly weren't interested, and I often ended up lecturing irritably about responsibility, sacrifice, and "doing God's work" from my driver's seat pulpit, which seemed to negate the whole point of the "cheerful giver." But I'm stubborn. And I don't like to fail. So I signed us up to hand out food and supplies at the food bank's distribution center in the city.

"I don't really feel like doing this," I whispered to Brad as he turned the minivan into the packed parking lot at the Center for People in Need. The wind bit through our winter jackets as the four of us scuttled toward the double doors of the warehouse, where we would distribute food to hundreds of people who would come through the line that night. I wanted to be home with a box of Cheez-Its and a glass of wine, my feet propped on the coffee table and *House Hunters* on the television screen.

Inside the cavernous room, Noah positioned himself next to a deep crate of potatoes. He quietly handed over one five-pound bag after another as a seemingly endless line of people pushed their carts past. One table down, Rowan distributed dented cans of kidney beans and SpaghettiOs with Brad. Meanwhile I offered heads of limp lettuce and loaves of wheat bread a day past expired.

I glanced up to glimpse an elderly Asian man accept a sack of potatoes from Noah and place it in his cart. I watched as the man stooped close and gently stroked my son's cheek with two fingers. He murmured something in a language I couldn't identify and then smiled widely at Noah, the skin around his eyes crinkling into deeply etched lines. The man rested his hand lightly on the crown of Noah's head for a moment before pushing his cart toward the next table.

Later Noah asked me what the man had said to him.

"I don't know," I answered. "I couldn't understand his language. I think it might have been Chinese. But I could tell he was really glad to see you. For some reason, you made him very happy."

I felt something stir in my heart when I witnessed that quiet exchange between my son and the elderly man in the food line. I saw something deeply and profoundly beautiful there, something I never expected to observe at a neighborhood food distribution center. I recognized God in the man's gentleness and joy, in his caress, in the way his eyes lit up when Noah smiled back at him, in the way his wrinkled, arthritic hand had rested for a few seconds on my son's head. It was a brief flash, but in that moment, God's presence was palpable and real. And I knew that leap of joy, that surge of emotion I felt in my heart was real too.

Back in 1995 astronomers decided to point the Hubble Space Telescope at a tiny patch of inky blackness no bigger than a grain of sand held out at arm's length. It was a risky move. The sliver of sky seemed to be devoid of any planets, stars, or galaxies. Observation time on the Hubble was costly and in high demand, and there was no guarantee the images produced would reveal anything more than utter emptiness.

Over a period of ten days, photons traveling thirteen billion years ended their journey on the detectors of the world's most powerful telescope, and when the images were processed, scientists were shocked by what was revealed. Light from more than three thousand previously undiscovered galaxies was illuminated in the images. Every miniscule spot, smear, and dot was an entire galaxy, each containing hundreds of billions of stars. In 2004 astronomers conducted a similar experiment, this time focusing the telescope on a patch of emptiness near the constellation Orion. Eleven days later, the processed images revealed another ten thousand previously undiscovered galaxies, an area of space that became known as the Hubble Ultra Deep Field. In both instances, it turned out there was a whole lot of something in what initially had looked like nothing at all.[5]

For me, the experience of leaping into community service was a little bit like the deep space experiment. Signing up to volunteer was a shot in the dark. I didn't know what to expect. I didn't know what I would discover—or even whether I would discover anything at all. I hoped to deepen my faith and to serve God in the process, but I wasn't at all sure either would happen.

I was surprised to find that over time, serving in my community began to shift me slowly and subtly from a purely intellectual kind of faith to a slightly more emotional belief. Tutoring, distributing food, and even the failed Meals on Wheels experience connected me with people in my community—people with whom I ordinarily wouldn't have had any contact at all. In doing so, these endeavors moved me from my own head, where I spent a copious amount of time analyzing and speculating about what constituted real faith, to a faith on the ground, in action, where I witnessed glimpses of God with my own eyes. These God-flashes were rare—Darveon's exuberant dance across the room; Len sitting straight and tall in his wheelchair, proudly showing Noah and Rowan the artwork that lined his apartment walls; two gnarled fingers stroking my son's cheek—but they were there. And while I couldn't verify these glimpses as proof of God in a double-blind scientific study and I didn't have any cold, hard evidence and the stamp of a reputable scientific journal to back my findings, my heart told me they were real just the same.

Frustrated by my lack of an emotionally charged belief, I could have given up altogether. I could have concluded that a "head faith," a faith devoid of much emotion, was as good as it was going to get for me. But I didn't. I continued to search for something more, something deeper. I leaped into volunteer work, what I thought might turn out to be nothing, and I found a glimpse of worlds of faith yet unexplored.

Sometimes, it seems, we need to press on, searching for and walking toward a destination we can't yet see. Sometimes we need to train our eyes on what initially looks like nothing at all. Those astronomers took a leap of faith when they focused the Hubble telescope on that patch of emptiness in the sky. They didn't know what, if anything, was out there. They had no idea what, if anything, that black patch of nothingness would reveal. They took a shot in the dark, and what they saw changed everything.

I'm glad I pressed on in search of a bit more light in the inky darkness. I'm grateful for the God-glimpses, the flashes of love and light I see when I connect in a real and meaningful way with my community. But at the same time, I know and accept that I may never be a cry-over-my-love-for-Jesus type of believer. I suspect I'm simply not put together that way. I have a pragmatic faith, a faith fueled by connection and service. And this is okay. At the risk of sounding cliché, faith takes all shapes and sizes; faith isn't a one-size-fits-all. The world needs the ones who weep for God, as well as the ones who don't but who still believe in him and love him in their own way.

8

Imperfect, Panicky Prayers

Everything that one turns in the
direction of God is prayer.

—IGNATIUS LOYOLA

The day I heard my pastor preach about cultivating a deeper, more interactive relationship with God, I knew I had a problem. *Great,* I thought as I sank lower in the pew. *Like it's not hard enough to believe in God. Now I actually have to work at connecting with him too?*

Frankly it was enough of a challenge to cultivate my marriage, a relationship with a real, live, breathing, conversing person who lived in my house. How in the world was I supposed to nurture an interactive relationship with God, someone I couldn't hear, see, touch, or feel? Someone I could talk to, but who didn't answer back (at least in words). On a positive note, I figured at least God wouldn't ask if, by chance, I was getting my period if I happened to get a little snarky with him.

I thought a lot about what Pastor Greg said that day, and I realized my prayer life came up far short. Truth be told, I had about as close a relationship with God as I had with Brenda, my tax accountant. The problem was, I didn't know how to relate to God, and I didn't have the foggiest idea how to begin.

When I was in sixth grade I read Judy Blume's teen novel *Are You There God? It's Me, Margaret* about a young girl struggling both with her faith and her burgeoning womanhood. Margaret talked to God as if he were her sister or her best friend, all casual and conversational about things such as menstrual periods, training bras, and boobs. I was horrified. *Who talks to God like that? Who talks to God like he is a regular person?* I thought. *Who is* that *comfortable with God?* I viewed Margaret as irreverent and rude, yet part of me envied her candor and comfort with God.

As a kid I wasn't taught to "talk" to God, but rather to confess—and not to God directly, but via my priest. I didn't actually converse with the priest either, and I certainly didn't sit with him face to face. I made my confession under cover of darkness within the confines of the dim confessional box, and then, ostensibly, the priest talked to God for me. At the time I wasn't exactly sure how it worked, whether the priest relayed my sins to God via his own prayer, or whether they were automatically conveyed to God simply by his hearing them, as if he were a confession conduit. Later I came to understand that it was the process of absolution at the confession's conclusion that freed me from my sins. Once the priest recited the prayer, "I absolve you of your sins in the name of the Father and the Son and the Holy Spirit. Amen," I was absolved of my sins, end of conversation.

While the details of the process were a bit muddled in my mind, one thing about it was clear to me, even as a second-grader making my first confession: the priest was my spokesperson, especially when it came to sinning and forgiveness. I never thought to ask God directly for forgiveness, to confess my sins straight to him. I always relied on the ritual of confession. I let the priest, not God himself, forgive my sins.

Aside from penance, I did not pray much as a kid. Occasionally I tossed up a desperation prayer: *PleaseGodpleaseGodletAndyaskmetothe dance.* Or the similar panic prayer: *PleaseGodpleaseGodpleaseGodlet mepassmath.* But there was no relationship with God, no conversing with him, no praying over tough decisions. Truthfully, when I was young, part of me even wished the practice of indulgences, which I learned about in eighth-grade history class, was still in vogue. It sounded like a pretty good deal to me: hand over a fistful of money, God turns a blind eye to your sins, and you live happily ever after in heaven. I cursed Martin Luther for ruining what seemed like a perfectly good arrangement.

As a kid, I went through the motions of religion mostly on autopilot. I adhered to the obligatory regimen of church attendance and confession in a desperate attempt to save myself from the depths of hell. But had I *wanted* to pray? Had I *wanted* to surrender to God? Had I *wanted* to try to listen to him? Of course not. I had not allowed myself the opportunity to *want to.* Three decades later when I heard Pastor Greg's message, I finally realized I had a choice. I could *choose* to want to have a relationship with God. God wasn't forcing me into a relationship with him the way my mom had compelled me to attend Mass. It was my decision.

On the other hand, the "have to" model suddenly seemed a whole lot easier. "Want to," like any relationship, required work. In his sermon, Pastor Greg compared our relationship with God to that of a thriving marriage. You can't expect to have a healthy relationship with your spouse if you talk to her once a week, he noted. Likewise praying once a week in church wouldn't amount to much of a relationship with God either.

The trouble was, I didn't really know how to pray. I worried I was doing it wrong. So often my prayers felt as dry as dust and empty of all meaning and emotion. When I did remember to pray, I barely managed to string together two coherent sentences. One minute I was earnestly asking God for patience with my children, the next minute—*oh shoot, I forgot to buy Parmesan cheese again.* Worse yet, I often fell asleep while praying, surely not what Jesus had in mind (although I found some consolation in reading about the disciples sleeping in the Garden of Gethsemane when they were supposed to be praying). More times than I could count, I'd be right in the middle of a prayer, and suddenly, without my even being aware of it, my thoughts would morph into that weird predream state that precedes sleep. I'd be thanking God for blessing me with the boys, and the next thing I knew, Noah and Rowan had transformed into alligators wearing purple-and-red-striped tube socks.

As a person who grew up on repetition and rote prayer, I also worried that some of my prayers, such as the Our Father, were so familiar they had become meaningless. I tried to concentrate on each word and phrase, determined to tap into their meaning, but often I found my mind wandering, hypnotized into a trance by the familiar words. I wondered if praying was really any use at all.

Despite my frustrations, the writer Kathleen Norris gave me hope that something was indeed happening under the surface. "I feel blessed to know from experience that it is in the act of worship, the act of saying and repeating the vocabulary of faith, that one can come to claim it as 'ours,'" wrote Norris in *Amazing Grace*. "It is in acts of repetition that seem senseless to the rational mind that belief comes, doubts are put to rest, religious conversion takes hold, and one feels at home in a community of faith."[1]

Over time I began to see prayer as a finely balanced line: while repetition and even mind-wandering were often a natural part of my prayers, such distraction didn't necessarily render my experience empty and meaningless. In fact, I came to discover a peace in the repetition, a respite for my analytical mind. Rather than holding each phrase of my prayer beneath a microscope, I relaxed into the rhythm of the words. While sometimes the result was indeed rote repetition, occasionally my prayer reared up, alive, each word drenched in explicit meaning and purposeful connection. It was the lighthouse flash of illumination again—just for a second my head and heart were working as one. Just for a second I was conversing with God.

Little by little I experimented with crafting my own prayers. At first it felt awkward. I didn't know what to say, beyond routine prayers for the people in my life who were ill or suffering in some way. Slowly, though, I grew more comfortable with God. And while I didn't speak to him like he was my sister or my best friend, my prayers began to relax from formality into a more conversational style.

I also got quite skilled at praying on the move. It wasn't always ideal, but more often than not, I uttered my prayers in haste while hurtling to Walgreens, my low-fat Starbucks mocha latte hold-the-whip-please sloshing into the cup holder, a kids' CD yodeling from the dashboard, Rowan methodically kicking my seat, and my cell phone blaring. When I admitted to an older woman in one of my Bible study classes that I often prayed on the run like this, she looked at me for a moment and then said quietly, "That's really too bad." I had no idea what she meant. Was she sorry my life was so hectic I was forced to resort to multitask praying? Or was she suggesting that prayer on the run was a ticket straight to hell? Her tone was friendly enough, but her words implied judgment. Or perhaps it was empathy. I wasn't sure how to respond, so I shrugged. That was the reality of my life, and I had to assume it was better than not praying at all.

I took some comfort from what Thomas Merton once said: "It is in the ordinary duties and labors of life that the Christian can and should develop his spiritual union with God."[2] Maybe praying in the car, in line at the grocery store, when the moment struck, was okay. Perhaps spirituality needn't be reserved solely for "sacred" moments, but woven into the fabric of the everyday. Maybe this was what Paul meant when he advised the Thessalonians, "Rejoice always, pray continually, give thanks in all circumstances" (1 Thessalonians 5:16–18).

Not long after I started to delve more into prayer, I had an experience that shook me to the core. It all began at the park, on an oddly warm day for early March in Nebraska. It was nearly seventy degrees, with a humid, fierce wind that spawned swirling dirt devils across the cracked cornfields. The air even smelled too warm, that earthy, wormy, ripe smell, an unsettling mix of growth and decay that usually descends pungently in mid-April or so. The park swarmed with kids and parents uncomfortably overdressed in jeans and cords, sweatshirts and fleece, all of us unwilling to relinquish our winter armor so early in the season. Everything about the afternoon felt off from the start—it was too warm, too windy, too bright. We squinted in the harsh, unfiltered light like groundhogs coming up for a sniff on February 2.

My friend Viviana and I sat together on a bench at the base of the slides as our five boys tore around the park. Viv's boys, Sam, Ben, and Eli, raced up two parallel slides, their worn sneakers wheeling round and round as they neared the top. Suddenly we heard a sharp voice. "Boys! Boys!" A fortyish woman pointed to the steps and barked, "You don't walk up the slides. You use the stairs. Don't let me see you do that again!"

"Well, that was a bit much," Viviana said quietly to me. I shrugged and rolled my eyes in agreement. Not three minutes later, less than ten feet in front of us, we saw the same woman suddenly grip Viviana's four-year-old sternly by the shoulders, bend down to his eye level, and shout, "You do not ever, ever push someone down the slide! Do you hear me? Do you hear me?!"

As the woman shook Eli's shoulder a little, Viviana leaped to her feet and ran toward them. "Hey! Hey! Get your hands off my son!" she shouted. "You don't speak to my son that way! He did not push your kid. I was sitting right here, and he did not push your kid!"

A shouting match erupted between the two women, and as the chaos rapidly unfolded, a man, evidently the woman's husband or boyfriend, pushed his way through the quieting crowd. His eyes were wide and white with fury, and he hurled obscenities as he moved toward Viv. Then he leaned in close and yelled at her, seething, spit gathering in the corners of his mouth and flying out with the spray of insults. Although she took one step back, Viviana didn't back down. She continued to defend Eli, insisting he hadn't pushed the woman's toddler, while the man continued to accost my friend. The kids froze in a rare moment of silence at the bottom of the slides.

It doesn't sound like much on paper, but in real time that afternoon at the playground, it was ugly and frightening.

And what was my reaction during all this, you might be wondering? Well, I'll tell you. I stood up. I rocked back and forth on the balls and heels of my feet. I paced a little and wrung my hands and looked at the man sitting on the next bench over from me. That's right. I did absolutely nothing. I stood and watched, rigid as a totem pole, while one of my closest friends was verbally attacked by two strangers at the park. Even Noah, sweet, quiet Noah, pretended to blast the angry couple with an imaginary water gun. "I'm spraying them away! I'm spraying the mean people away!" he yelled, making emphatic gushing noises as I frantically shushed him. But I did nothing. It was "a scene," and I felt a visceral repulsion clench deep in my stomach. Not only did I not want to get involved, not only was I afraid and leery of the confrontation, I was embarrassed. I pretended I wasn't with Viviana because I didn't want anything to do with the ugliness transpiring at the bottom of the slides.

Later, shaken and humiliated, Viviana wept in the driver's seat of her car as I stood at the window, stammering and consoling. I was mortified. I didn't know what to say and was too ashamed to explain my puzzling lack of response. I had disappointed my friend. I had betrayed her.

I could not get over it. For two full days I replayed the scene over and over in my mind, ashamed by my lack of courage and loyalty. At playgroup when a mutual friend murmured empathetically, "I heard what happened at the park," I hung my head and then did what I do best when faced with an awkward situation: I self-deprecatingly joked about my lack of response, acting out a hyperbolic imitation of myself wringing my hands and pacing.

I did what I could to redeem myself. I called to check on Viv and apologized profusely while she graciously glossed over the details and downplayed my role, insisting it was no big deal. But I couldn't forgive myself. Why was I such a loser? Why was I so fearful of confrontation? Why did I choose inaction over friendship and loyalty? What kind of Christian was I, if I couldn't even defend the "weak" at a Lincoln playground?

All I could think of was the infamous case of Kitty Genovese, the woman stabbed to death in a Queens apartment building in 1964 as a dozen neighbors listened yet did nothing, neighbors who were aware that an attack was taking place yet remained completely unresponsive. The Genovese case prompted research into a social psychology phenomenon called the "bystander effect," which suggests that the greater the number of witnesses to a crime, the less likely one of those witnesses will intervene.

The theory seemed to hold true that afternoon in the park. Although there were dozens of parents around the swings and the slides that day, not one stepped forward to help settle the dispute. Everyone reacted as I did, by looking away or suddenly becoming very involved with their own children. But the fact that I was one of many who didn't react was little consolation. After all, Viviana was my friend, not a mere stranger.

Finally, two full days after the ugly incident, I remembered God. I remembered God was with me, even in my worst moments of weakness, most especially in my worst moments of weakness. I remembered

God wouldn't abandon me as I had abandoned Viviana. I remembered God didn't recoil from messy, ugly situations and wouldn't turn away from me, even when I made bad choices. And so, two days after the horrible incident in the park, I finally did what I should have done from the get-go: I prayed. *Dear God,* I said. (I always start my prayers this way, like I am writing a letter to my great-aunt Caroline.) *Please help me. Please give me the courage to stand up to people. Please help me forgive myself. Please don't let Viviana tell everyone what a loser I am. Please give me strength. Amen.*

It took two days, but I had finally remembered to pray. It was belated and groveling and a little bit pathetic, but it was a real, authentic prayer. I had talked to God. And I believe he listened.

My goal, of course, was to make prayer a constant presence in my life, a natural inclination rather than an afterthought on a two-day delay cycle. I wanted to learn how to "pray continually" rather than making it a formal ritual or, worse, a mindless habit wedged into a specific slot in my day. I wanted prayer to become my first instinct rather than my last.

Not long after the park incident, Brad, the boys, and I went on a daylong canoe trip in the Boundary Waters of northern Minnesota. I should preface this story by telling you straight up that I am not a canoeist. Prior to this outing I had canoed twice in my entire life, both times when Brad and I were first *dating.* Need I say more? But Brad wanted to take the kids on a little adventure while we were in

Minnesota, and I wasn't going to be the stuffed shirt who stayed back at the cabin alone.

We wove around lily pads and over golden grasses that undulated like ribbons beneath the surface, our paddles dipping rhythmically in and out of the water. Noah admired the lavender iris springing from the edges of the marshy shore. Rowan threw Goldfish crackers into the water for the walleyes. After about two hours of easy paddling, we pulled the canoe onto an island and portaged (wilderness-speak for lugged bulky canoe across dry land while being viciously attacked by mosquitoes the size of whooping cranes) to the other side. As we rounded the corner on the far side of the island, we were surprised to find ourselves nearly knocked flat by a gale-force wind. Somehow what had been a barely perceptible breeze at our backs had escalated to what felt like Hurricane Andrew.

Brad and I secured the kids' life vests and we all plunged in. As we pushed off the rocks with our paddles, it took about thirty seconds for me to realize that the return trip was not going to be relaxing. Though I was paddling as hard as I could, when I glanced at the shore, it wasn't moving at all; we were literally paddling in place. To make matters worse, the water was no longer gently lapping but was instead gushing over the bow in a torrent, and every few minutes the canoe threatened to turn broadside against the waves. If you've ever canoed in a large lake, you know this was a dangerous situation.

"Michelle! Michelle!" Brad yelled over the wind from the stern. "You've got to paddle faster, paddle harder! The canoe has got to stay against the waves. We can't get broadsided!"

The kids were terrified, and so was I (not sure about Brad; he doesn't let on in situations such as this). When I looked over my shoulder, Noah was clutching the sides of the canoe with a steely grip, his eyes wide as if he were witnessing the Loch Ness monster rear out of the lake. Meanwhile Rowan was screaming over and over, "We're all gonna die! We're all gonna die!"

I tried to console them. "No, no, no, everything's okay. We're going to be just fine," I yelled over my shoulder. "It's just a little wavy, that's all!" The problem was, you can't speak soothingly in gentle tones in a thirty-mile-per-hour wind. As I screamed reassurances, my voice pinched and shrill, the kids looked even more terrified.

And that's when I prayed. I'll admit, it was a combination of cursing and praying, but that was progress. A year or two prior, it would have been entirely cursing under my breath. So when I wasn't blasting Brad in my head—*Stupid, stupid idea. Mr. Stupid Nature Man dragging us out here in this stupid wilderness...*—I was praying, *Please God, please God, please don't let the canoe turn over; please help us get to shore safely; please give me the strength to keep paddling; please keep my children safe.* I even thought about suggesting to the kids that we pray out loud together. But I ditched that idea when I realized it probably would have panicked them further. "What?! Mommy's praying? Mommy's praying! We're all gonna die!!"

We made it to shore. I lived to tell about it and complain about it. And I realized two things in the aftermath of our adventure. One: I was seriously lacking upper-body strength, so much so that turning the knob on the car radio dial required two hands (one hand to turn the dial and the other to brace the arm of the hand turning the dial) for a full week after the canoe trip. And two: I could turn to God and

I *would* turn to God in a time of distress. While I couldn't definitively prove God had answered my prayer—I couldn't say for sure whether he had affected our circumstances or whether we'd safely made it to shore all on our own—I'd found comfort and relief in trusting him.

My most difficult prayer moment came not long after the canoe incident, when I was asked to pray aloud for the first time in a group setting. Through my church, I had joined a small group that met on Friday nights—the fact that I enrolled in a Friday night Bible study should tell you a lot about my social life—to read and discuss a spiritual book together. This time the topic was prayer.

I'd never intended to join a small group. My pastor had mentioned it when we were chatting after a Sunday service, and I had said something vague like, "Yeah, I should join one of those sometime." I'd simply been making small talk, with absolutely no intention of following through. But Pastor Sara took me at my word, and within a week, I had an invitation in my in-box from Kim, a small-group leader. I accepted, but only because I felt like the pastor herself had invited me.

I liked the group members—I truly did. But despite everyone's congeniality, to me, the whole concept seemed like a recipe for social discomfort. Something about small-group Bible study feels inherently forced and awkward. Think about it. You take a handful of people who don't know one another well, foist Bibles on them, plunk down a plate of brownies, and instruct them to discuss (the Bible, not the brownies). Plus, my husband, the stoic Minnesota "I don't talk about my feelings with people I don't know" Lutheran, refused to attend. So I was on my own.

To further complicate matters, our second assignment suggested we conclude our discussion with prayer. I was somewhat accustomed to this ritual from other church classes I'd taken. What I didn't antici-pate was Kim's suggestion that we *individually* share a prayer. *Out loud.* To her credit, Kim emphasized that we shouldn't feel forced or even compelled to pray aloud; we should only participate if we were comfortable with it. Nevertheless I was horrified. Honestly, if I had suspected when I enrolled that praying aloud was even a possibility, I would have tucked my Bible beneath my arm and headed for the hills. I couldn't fathom anything more uncomfortable, more awkward, more bizarre than praying aloud with this group of acquaintances. I didn't pray aloud with anyone for that matter—not with my mother, not with my husband, not with our pet fish. Really, could there be anything more dreadful than praying out loud in a group? I would have preferred a root canal. A bikini wax. Both at the same time. Pretty much anything over praying out loud.

The closest I'd ever come to a similar experience was each night at bedtime when I sped through the obligatory "family prayer" with Noah and Rowan, eager to snap off the bedside lamp and skip down the stairs to watch *House Hunters*. Well, that and saying grace before dinner, a treasured family practice that I resurrected biennially. Or when the pastor was coming to dinner.

One time, before inviting Pastor Sara for dinner, we practiced saying grace with the boys for seven nights straight and had it down pretty well. The night of the dinner, as we bowed our heads and folded our hands, Noah blurted, "Oh! We're saying a prayer! Mommy forgets to do that. A lot." This was, in fact, a profound understatement (although I'm not sure why I was the sole parent taking the hit).

"That happens to everyone once in a while," Pastor Sara acknowledged generously, clearly seeing through our transparent eleventh-hour attempt to introduce prayer into the mealtime ritual.

Anyway, that was one time with one pastor, in the privacy and comfort of my own home; this, on the other hand, was a whole group of people, nearly strangers, gathered in a circle in Kim's living room. Once again, I fought the flight instinct, weighing whether or not I could spend the entire prayer time in the bathroom with the water running. Before I could even decide, though, Kim graciously began to pray, and one by one each group member took a turn. Amanda prayed for patience; Deepa for peace in the world; Nicole for help in slowing her frenetic pace; Drew for guidance in his job. As one prayer blended into the next, I wasn't listening to any of it. No, I was far too paralyzed by fear to tune in, let alone pray along. Even worse, it was nearly impossible to determine whether a person had concluded his or her prayer or was merely pausing contemplatively. Just when I thought Drew was finally done, just as I inhaled a shaky breath and geared up for my own public prayer, he launched a fresh litany of requests. *For the love of the land, wrap it up, man. You're killing me here,* I thought irritably, before realizing that not only was I not praying, I was also actually *sinning* in the process.

When Drew finally exhausted his prayer, I was left shuddering like a quaking aspen. And then an interminable pause yawned open as they waited, serene and expectant, hands clasped, eyes closed. My heart palpitated; I clenched and unclenched my fists and worked myself into a frothing frenzy as I stole glances at everyone. No one even looked clammy. No one even peeked. I know because I wasn't pray-ing...I was spying on them, peering at their bowed heads through half-closed eyes.

I couldn't do it. I sat there spying while people shifted in their seats, the silence pressing into my chest, the furnace whirring distantly in the bowels of the house. Someone sniffed. The silence was insuffer-able, yet I still didn't speak. I was too afraid—afraid I would stutter and stumble. Afraid I wouldn't pray for the "right" things. Afraid I wouldn't sound appropriately prayerful. Finally, after what felt like two days, Kim closed with the Lord's Prayer, and I nearly swooned off the couch with relief. I was the only one in our group who hadn't prayed out loud. I kid you not, the pray-aloud session that night lasted nearly twenty minutes. *Labor* was less painful. I suspect delivering quintuplets would have been less painful. I went home, uncorked a bottle of Shiraz, accosted Brad for abandoning me to a bunch of pray-out-louders, and declared that I was never going back.

Of course I went back the following Friday, but I drank the Shiraz *before* I went. This time, Kim tactfully suggested we go around the circle and casually talk about what we *might* pray for on the off chance we were given the opportunity to pray. This, though clearly a semantic trick, eased my discomfort. This I could do. There was no "heavenly Father," no "and this we pray in Jesus's name"; it was just plain old conversation. With our eyes open. It seemed like we were talking, rather than praying. And that made all the difference.

"Well, *if* I were to pray right now, this is what I *might* pray for...," I said when my turn came. Ah, the beauty of the disclaimer. One linguistic twist, and I suddenly felt unencumbered, free to rattle off a dozen items that I would perhaps pray for, given the opportunity:

patience with my kids, better mothering, my friend in Boston who was out of work, a coworker on bed rest, less coveting, less swearing, more generosity, more faith, perhaps a miracle or two. They could not shut me up.

That experience of "praying" aloud helped me understand what it was exactly about praying, even silent praying, that intimidated me. I typically approached God as I would a CEO—politely and respectfully, but on guard. I felt as if I needed to be on my best behavior with God. I didn't know how to talk to him like he was an intimate friend or a beloved parent. "Praying" aloud with my small group, painful though it was, helped me realize that I could talk to God as I did my closest friends and family—honestly and trustfully. I didn't have to use fancy words or elaborate expressions. I didn't have to worry about being too long-winded or too brief. In fact, I didn't really need to be concerned about the style or even the substance of my prayers at all.

I began to realize, as Ignatius Loyola once said, that anything I turned in the direction of God was a prayer. It took me a long time, but I finally began to understand that I didn't need to impress God with perfect words, fully articulated thoughts, and catchy phrases. God didn't need me to come to him as someone else. He didn't need me to dress up my prayers in poetry or lace them with special, sacred words. He wanted me, the rambling, bumbling, awkward me. The misfit me. Mumbling and chanting, begging and pleading, thanksgiving and praise, petition, song, gesture, breath, and even wordless attention—all were ways to turn in the direction of God. All were prayers.

It didn't matter a bit that my prayers didn't sound like anyone else's. God wanted to hear from me. The real me.

9

Taking a
Mulligan...Again

Man is born broken.
He lives by mending.
The grace of God is glue.
—EUGENE O'NEILL

Joining a small group, getting more comfortable with prayer, and digging into the Bible with greater frequency were all practices that moved me along the faith continuum, but I was still stumped by a theological concept mentioned again and again in church and in the Bible: grace.

I remember the Sunday my church launched a sermon and study series called CrossWalk. Based on John Ortberg's book *Fully Devoted: Living Each Day in Jesus' Name,* the initiative was designed to help us integrate worship into our everyday lives. I thought it sounded like a great spiritual growth opportunity. And it was...on paper. In reality, it nearly killed me.

Part one of the plan suggested we praise God throughout the

course of our day. The first few hours were a snap. I praised God left and right. I thanked him for the golden ginkgo tree silhouetted against the blue sky. I praised him for curbing my desire to run Mr. BMW in his hotshot shades off the road after he veered into my lane and cut me off, causing me to splash mocha latte on my new off-white, boot-cut cords. I thanked God for two boys who make me laugh and a husband who fixes my coffee every morning, even though he never touches the stuff himself.

But the trouble was, the day was long. Not counting slumber, we're talking sixteen hours or so. And who could praise God for sixteen hours straight? By the time seven o'clock rolled around, my nerves were frayed like an old hair elastic, and I'd resorted to Darth Vader deep-breathing. While I barked orders—"Finish your snack! Pick out a book!"—and tried to rein in the spiraling chaos, the kids got giddy as kids do when bedtime looms, wheeling around the living room like bumblebees on speed, ricocheting off furniture, bouncing on the couch like rubber superballs, and throwing Cheez-Its at each other.

Before I realized what was happening, I morphed from a thinly disguised insane woman trying desperately to act like Jesus into a stark raving madwoman; Jesus cast aside like a rumpled Halloween costume, as Medusa with a head full of writhing snakes slid into his place. In a span of thirty seconds, I grabbed a handful of Cheez-Its, crunched them in my fist, and threw them at Rowan, orange crumbs cascading like sprinkles off his carrot-top head. (Note: this is actually an effective strategy for summoning shocked silence and a total cessation of pre-bedtime lunacy, but I advise to use it sparingly.) I rattled off a list of lost privileges rivaling a day at Guantánamo Bay—"No books! No snacks! No story! No snuggling! No prayers!" (Yes, I took away prayers.) Then I dropped each boy howling and sniveling into his respective bed. And burst into tears myself.

Yes, this was how I launched CrossWalk. This was how I integrated worship into my everyday life. This was how I glorified God with my thoughts and actions. It went really well. Oh, and I should mention, it was also my husband's birthday. Happy birthday, honey, from your raving lunatic Medusa wife.

I'm guessing Jesus probably would not have hurled snacks at his disciples, no matter how exasperated he was with their constant vying for position and their proclivity for sleeping in the Garden of Gethsemane. He also probably would not have forbidden prayer as a disciplinary measure.

While I wept on Brad's shoulder, complaining pitifully that my CrossWalk was a bust, he assured me with compassion and genuine affection that I could try again: "Honey, it's okay, really. You can start again tomorrow; you did really well during the first part of the day, didn't you? It's not a complete loss." (Of course *he* managed to be like Jesus with no problem.)

I did pick up one pointer from my abysmal one-day CrossWalk experiment. I learned to take a mulligan, as they say in golf. I don't actually play golf, but Brad does, and he's explained the concept of a mulligan to me, which is essentially a do-over. If your drive goes awry and your ball plunks into the pond, you can take a mulligan. Grace, it turned out, was like a mulligan, the chance to take another shot, to start over again. I had received a mulligan, grace, from God (and my husband and children) when I morphed into Medusa and threw Cheez-Its at Rowan. I received the chance to start over the next day and the day after that. That's what Brad tried to tell me as I wept on his shoulder, bemoaning the fact that I'd ruined my chance to be a good Christian, along with ruining his birthday. The problem was, I didn't really get it. I didn't understand the concept of grace yet. And it would take awhile before I did.

Not long after the Cheez-It incident I took Rowan with me to the grocery store. Rowan typically allowed me about half the time I needed to grocery shop properly for the week before plunging into full tantrum mode. I could never anticipate what would set him off. One week it was the chilly gallon of milk brushing against his calf. The next week the fact that no, I absolutely would not let him take home the towering ficus tree on sale for $9.99. Often I was able to stave off the inevitable for a few minutes with a quick trip through the bakery department. Each week I wooed Rowan with a frosted cookie and tried to avoid the judgmental glances of the mothers with their properly behaved, ringletted girls, who sat like Cabbage Patch Kids and munched organic peach slices. I always held out hope for the day I would exit Super Saver with a cart full of groceries and both Rowan and my dignity intact.

This, as I recall, was not that week. My hopes crumbled to bits in the cracker aisle. As I mulled over the forty-nine varieties of Wheat Thins, I heard a thin, quavering voice down the aisle: "Oh, you'd better be careful, young man. You don't want to hurt yourself now, do you? Is that your mommy down there?" My head snapped in their direction, and I saw Rowan, one leg flung over the side of the cart, arms splayed, balancing his plump little body on the metal edge like a skydiver hurtling toward Earth. A sixty-fiveish woman wearing eyeglasses as big and round as owl eyes stared at me reproachfully as she spoke to my son.

Now nothing makes my blood boil like passive-aggressive accusations of my being a negligent and irresponsible mother. Even when I am, in fact, being a negligent and irresponsible mother. Worse yet, Owl Spectacles then did something completely unforgivable: she romanticized motherhood. "I sure wish my kids were that age again," she said wistfully. "I really do miss it, and it all goes by so fast. You make sure to appreciate this, young lady, because someday it will all be gone."

Really? So someday I might actually be entitled to take a full, uninterrupted nine seconds to decide whether I would rather try the Zesty Salsa or the Smoky BBQ Wheat Thins? She was saying someday my bananas would not be mashed on the bottom of my cart, stomped to a pulp by little feet by the time I rolled sweating and flushed through the checkout line? Someday I wouldn't have to explain to a wailing child why he could not, in fact, lick the shrink-wrapped package of sirloin? She was telling me that someday I would not have all this? I wasn't sure I could bear such loss.

"Really, lady," I wanted to say, "can you not see that I am just a hair, just the teeniest hair away from a full-scale meltdown? Can you not see that I have gulped a few too many sips of Starbucks this morning, that I am a little bit maniacal, that I may, in fact, start heaving huge sobs right here in the middle of the cracker aisle?"

Clearly she could not see that.

What I really wanted to do in that moment was grab an armload of Dr Pepper two-liters off the shelf and start rolling them at Owl Spectacles' feet. And then I wanted to shake her (gently) by the shoulders and demand, "Do you really miss this? Really?" Instead, I sighed loudly and mumbled inaudibly, "I know it. You're right. This is just.

So. Special." And then I turned and pushed my cart and Rowan in the opposite direction.

This was the clincher: I truly believed in that moment that if it were not for other people, I could have been a good Christian. I believed that if it had been just me and, say, the birds and the squirrels, I would have done okay. I thought I could be a good Christian among animals. But it was people—people with their comments and their judgments and their good intentions—who taxed my ability to behave as I should. My fellow human beings made the whole Christian attitude thing very, very difficult to achieve.

That day in Super Saver I felt as though Owl Spectacles had single-handedly thwarted me. *She* made me fantasize about rolling soda bottles like bowling balls down the aisle at her on a Tuesday morning. *She* made me imagine, just for a split second, a scenario in which she stepped into the parking lot and was flattened by a train of grocery carts. My moral failure was *her* fault.

The hardest lesson I learned postconversion was that I was not instantly reformed. I'd assumed I would instantly become a new and improved Michelle, as if I'd stepped into a Faith Makeover Machine and exited with a cute bob, radiant highlights, and a brand-new Jesus-like attitude. But that wasn't the case. The fact that I'd had a conversion experience—albeit one that was evolving at a glacial pace—didn't mean that I had automatically and instantaneously become nicer, more forgiving, more tolerant, less gossipy, more patient. My choice to believe—cautiously—in God didn't mean I no longer fantasized on occasion about rolling soda bottles down the supermarket aisle at an elderly lady. My newfound faith didn't prevent me from morphing into a snake-haired mother who tossed crunched-up Cheez-Its at her child. I was disappointed to find I was the same old whiny ingrate I had been yesterday. The same snipey, catty girl. The same eye-rolling wife. The same grumpy grocery shopper. The same sometimes-bored mom.

I slowly and painfully learned that my conversion was not to be a one-time, road-to-Damascus experience, but rather, as the Benedictines say, a *conversatio morum:* a "conversion of life," a daily, even minute-by-minute decision to continue walking the path. My warm-heart conversion experience was the easy part. It was the "conversion of life," the living it day in and day out, that was the challenge. I had to work at it, and let God work on me, one infinitesimal step at a time.

In her book *Amazing Grace,* Kathleen Norris acknowledged what she calls a "basic and valuable truth about conversion." We don't magically transform into new people, shedding our faults like dirty clothes. What happens, says Norris, is much more subtle.

> In the process of conversion, the detestable parts of our selves do not vanish so much as become transformed. We can't run from who we are, with our short tempers, our vanity, our sharp tongues, our talents for self-aggrandizement, self-delusion, or despair. But we can convert, in its root meaning of turn around, so that we are forced to face ourselves as we really are. We can pray that God will take our faults and use them for the good.[1]

This, observed Norris, reveals God's mercy in a way that a magical, instantaneous transformation cannot.

When I read Norris's thoughts about conversion, I realized she had nailed an important but simple fact: I was not perfect, either as a nonbeliever or as a believer. Although Jesus asked me to be perfect, I could not achieve perfection, simply because I was not him. This was hard for me to accept. As a Type A overachiever I don't like to fail. In fact, I saw little appeal in the idea of embracing a challenge I knew in advance I would fail, which is the reality of my life as a would-be follower of Jesus.

Herein lay the conundrum. I knew I would inevitably stray from my spiritual path, yet I had to keep striving, fully aware that I would flounder and flail and feel like I was drowning. I couldn't give up because I knew now that failure was an integral part of the transformation process. And I also knew that, ultimately, I would survive and thrive and, with God's intervention, become a nicer, more humble, more patient, less gossipy, slightly more Jesus-like person. On some days.

One Presidents' Day I took my kids to the mall to kill a few hours, and as I sat in the play area, I recognized the most beautiful mom at Rowan's preschool sitting across from me. I am not exaggerating when I say this woman stops traffic. The first time I saw her was the night of preschool orientation, when all heads turned as she sashayed into the room. The dads were visibly taken, the moms visibly shaken. Clearly the women in the room were thinking the same thing: *Great. And now on top of everything else in my life, I have to look at* her *every day? That's just fabulous.* Meanwhile, you could almost see the wheels turning in the dads' heads: *I just may be able to swing pickup a couple of afternoons a week after all.*

For starters this woman was model tall and rail thin. *How in the world,* I wondered, as I sat across from her at the play area, *could that svelte wisp of a body have grunted out a red-faced, bawling infant and then reverted to its prebaby glory?* No pear bulged the sides of her jeans; no muffin top peeked from beneath her shirt; no chicken wings flapped on the undersides of her slender arms. Had they sucked her newborn out through her ear canal? And it got worse. Her hair shimmered, brushing the luscious eyelashes of her round doe eyes and cascading in a platinum waterfall across her shoulders. Her skin was Gwyneth Paltrow–flawless. Her makeup was Jessica Alba–professional. She wore 7 For All Mankind jeans—who in the world wears those to the mall play area in Lincoln, Nebraska, for heaven's sake? She looked like a goddess.

I, by contrast, was wearing five-year-old frumpster yoga pants, the ones that had never witnessed an actual downward dog. The ones with the unraveling hem. The ones that clung to my thighs in a tenacious declaration of love, yet drooped in the rear, clearly unwilling to commit. To complete the look, I wore a pilly turquoise fleece sweatshirt, static-clinging like Saran Wrap to my sports bra–flattened chest, and brand-new, brightly glowing running shoes. Not the Nike Air Pegasus+; mine were New Balance, on sale at Kohl's. My hair was not dyed. In fact, my hair was not even washed. And I was not wearing a lick of makeup, my ghastly February pallor exaggerated by the pronounced age spot on my right cheek and the I-am-middle-aged-and-have-adult-acne zit on my chin.

Only Rowan's crying forced me to tear my eyes from the Goddess, and when I did, I saw that he was being mercilessly terrorized by a girl more than twice his age and size. As he tried to slip his roly-poly, little body down a miniature slide, the girl perched atop the structure like the Queen of Sheba, jabbing him with her feet and sending him tumbling onto the floor. One glance at the girl, with her button nose, beribboned hair, and Hanna Andersson striped tights and sweater, and I knew, without a moment's hesitation, that she was the Child of the Goddess.

I declung my fleece, sauntered over, and kindly told the girl that she was behaving inappropriately. She looked at me with haughty disdain, the look of a girl who knew her mom was the Goddess and she was on her way to becoming one too. Heaven help me, I wanted to wring her sweet neck. But I didn't. Instead, I declung my fleece and yoga pants and returned to my seat, glancing at the Goddess to gauge her reaction to the confrontation. She hadn't noticed a thing, of course—she was too busy chatting on her fuchsia polka-dot cell phone and flipping her golden hair.

No sooner had I reseated my frumpiness when I glanced over and saw Hanna Anderwench torturing my son again. This time she gazed directly at me as her striped stocking feet pummeled Rowan off the slide. Rowan looked at me expectantly. So again I rearranged the cling, sauntered over, and whispered to Hannawench, "Don't you dare touch him again or you are going to be in big trouble." I used my fiercest This Mommy Means Business voice, and still, she could not give a hoot. She gazed back at me, serene and unflummoxed. And as I gathered my cling and my pear thighs and my howling kids and stalked past the Goddess, I noticed she, too, didn't give a hoot, still giggling into her cell phone and stroking her blond beauty, while her monstrous daughter tortured my kid.

I fumed in my head all the way home. *Stupid wenchbag pretty girl and your stupid pretty kid. Why don't you get your glamour-girl face out of your compact and pay attention to what's happening?* I was ruthless, my self-righteousness boiling over like lava. *I may be a frumpbag, I may be wearing stupid white sneakers with hideous black yoga pants that fit five years ago, but at least I watch my kids. Wenchbag.* The tirade inside my head proceeded for ten minutes or so, until I realized, with profound certainty, that Jesus was not happy with my behavior.

I suspected Jesus would not use the word *wenchbag* fourteen times in ten minutes to describe a mother and her daughter. I also guessed Jesus would not care much that the Goddess was wearing 7 For All Mankind jeans that molded like a glove to her rounded size-two rear end. I also figured Jesus wouldn't even care that the Goddess's child was impeccably dressed, while mine both had McDonald's chicken nugget honey mustard sauce dribbled on their shirts. No, Jesus would not care about any of that.

What he did care about, I knew, was the fact that I had judged the Goddess purely on her looks and that I was seething with envy over the fact that she looked like a goddessy Gwyneth Paltrow, while I resembled a less svelte version of Richard Simmons. I recognized that Jesus cared about the fact that I had ruthlessly judged her for one neglectful mommy moment, when I myself had committed dozens of similar transgressions in the last week alone. I realized he cared about the fact that I had also turned my wrath on her child, who, though decidedly bratty, was just a bored kid trying to entertain herself. Jesus cared that my ire was fueled primarily by the fact that she was the daughter of Gwyneth Goddess, while my kids were stuck with Mother Simmons.

This is so hard; why does this have to be so difficult? I complained to myself in the car. *Why can't we just love the ugly people? Why can't we*

just love the poor, underprivileged people? Isn't it enough to love the frumpy
bums? Do we have to love the goddessy Gwyneth Paltrows too? Why does
God insist we love everyone, *even the pretty, rich people? Why does God*
have to be so inclusive?

By the time we arrived home, I had apologized, in my mind, to
the Goddess for my searing judgment. While I was at it, I apologized
to God, too, and asked him for a little more help in the self-righteousness, envy, and coveting departments. And then I took a good hard
look at myself and realized something shocking. It wasn't the "other
people" who inhibited my ability to be a good Christian. It was me. It
wasn't everyone else's fault; it was my own fault. I took my issues—my
insecurities as a mother, my insecurities about my droopy bum, my
insecurities about the behavior of my children and how their behavior
reflected on me—and I foisted them onto everyone else, onto the
Goddess and the Goddess Child and even onto old Owl Spectacles.

As I sat in my driveway, gripping the steering wheel with both
hands, this knowledge slunk into the pit of my stomach and slowly
filled up my whole insides. I just sat in the minivan for a few minutes
with the kids in the backseat, oozing self-disgust, repulsed by my own
inability to be a decent Christian, or even a decent person for that matter. And then I did something that in the past would have been un-
thinkable. I forgave myself. I gave myself a do-over, a mulligan, a
chance to do it right the next time. I accepted God's grace. As Kathleen Norris said, I turned around. I put my faults—my insecurities,
my judgments, my self-righteousness—right out there and faced them
head on. And then I gave God a chance to help me turn my faults into
something good.

A few days later I saw the Goddess again at Rowan's preschool. As I stood next to her outside the classroom door and exchanged pleasantries about the weather, I realized something right away. I liked the Goddess. She was instantly likable: warm, chatty, easy to talk to, genuine. The kind of person I would want for a friend. And when she flashed her professionally whitened smile at me, I gratefully grinned back, grace passing over me like a warm wave.

That was grace. The limitless mulligan. The ultimate do-over. The infinite second chance. I may have failed to love the Goddess and Owl Spectacles and a whole host of other people, but God would give me another opportunity, and another and another. Day in and day out. He would work with me, and he would work through me. And he would never, ever give up on me.

C. S. Lewis said the only way to get a quality—like patience or kindness or generosity—was to start behaving like you had that particular quality already. To behave as if you were patient, kind, or generous before you actually were patient, kind, or generous, he reasoned, was the very beginning, the start of your collaboration with God. Acting, even pretending, Lewis argued, eventually led to the real deal. In that moment of pretending, Lewis said, God was at your side, beginning, "to turn you into the same kind of thing as Himself...beginning, so to speak, to 'inject' His kind of life and thought...into you; beginning to turn the tin soldier into a live man."[2]

Lewis was right, I realized. Sometimes I had to fake it. I had to behave as a "good Christian" before I actually was a "good Christian" in reality. Sometimes I had to go through the motions before the real transformation took place.

Once again, that lesson was learned in a grocery store. As I stood in the aisle quietly relishing the luxury of a child-free shopping excursion, an elderly lady maneuvered her wheezing electronic minicart over to where I stood and interrupted my reverie. "Excuse me, miss," she inquired softly. "Would you mind handing me one of those beef broths, the Always Save brand, please, if you wouldn't mind?"

I passed her the can, and we made small talk about the weather. And then, as we met in each subsequent aisle, I handed over more items she needed—a bag of brown sugar, a jar of sugar-free strawberry jam, a box of toothpaste. We continued the thread of conversation, chatting about the price of groceries and gas, our favorite breakfast foods, how chilly the freezer section was.

I left Super Saver smug and satisfied, marveling over my kindness, patience, helpfulness, and goodwill. *Wasn't I just so good, so very much like Jesus in there?* I thought as I pushed the grocery cart toward my car. *You know, I think I'm really getting this Jesus thing.*

But as I heaved my groceries into the back of my minivan I was struck with a devastating realization. There I was, puffed up like a blowfish in the Super Saver parking lot, yet what had I done? Besides handing over a couple cans of broth and a tube of toothpaste, absolutely nothing. Come to think of it, I hadn't even waited to see if she needed help at the register. Super Saver was one of those bag-your-own warehouse stores; how was she going to manage that from her squatty electronic cart? How would she squeeze those plastic bags brimming with broth cans into her cart's tiny wire basket? What if she fell? What if she broke a hip? What if the strain of lifting the bags of broth brought on a heart attack or a stroke?

I sat trapped in my Chevy Venture with the motor running, sweat pooling in my bra despite the air conditioning. I couldn't retrace my steps in search of her; it was ninety-eight degrees, and my Skinny Cow chocolate peanut butter ice cream sandwiches would melt into a puddly mess in minutes if I turned off my car.

So I sat.

And then I drove, circling the parking lot to scope out cars in the handicapped spaces. There were only two—a dusty Oldsmobile, its beige rear jutting awkwardly into the lane, and an elegant silver Cadillac Eldorado. I slid into a spot a few spaces down from the Olds—she had seemed more Oldsmobile material in her floral dress and sensible shoes. And then I waited, my eyes glued to the Super Saver exit. I was now stalking Mrs. Beef Broth, hoping to redeem myself by at least loading her groceries into the trunk.

Finally I saw her, wobbling on a three-pronged cane, peony-pink housecoat snapping in the wind, bulky purse banging up against her stockings. Next to her was an elderly man, his pants pulled high and cinched well with a belt, a fedora pulled jauntily over his forehead. Mrs. Beef Broth slipped an arm through his, and together they pushed the cart deliberately toward the beige Oldsmobile. I pulled out of the parking lot, smiling.

God had been right there in the Super Saver parking lot, turning pretense into reality, injecting himself into me. He nudged me from the black and white of right and wrong, from the "I should" and the "I'm supposed to" to the "I want to." He illuminated my smug pride and vanity, making it all too clear that I had been motivated at least in part by selfishness and a need to "do good" in order to satisfy my own ego. He suggested I stay in the parking lot while my romaine wilted and my Skinny Cows sweated, waiting to reach out, to connect. I had pretended to have grace and humility as I handed groceries over to Mrs. Beef Broth in the Super Saver aisles. But in pretending, in going through the motions, I ultimately reached genuine intent, if only for a moment. I had only scratched the surface of sacrifice in the store, but in the parking lot, as I sat and waited, forfeiting my own time (not to mention the freshness of my lettuce) to help another human being, I experienced real grace. In the store I had offered assistance because it was the "right thing to do." In the parking lot, I waited to help because I wanted to, out of a genuine love for my fellow neighbor. It didn't matter that Mrs. Beef Broth hadn't needed my help. I had been injected with God, as C. S. Lewis would say, in the Super Saver parking lot, of all places. His life flowed into me, transforming the tin soldier into a genuine person with a living, beating heart.

For a long time I equated grace with the prayer offered prior to the Thanksgiving feast. Slowly, I began to realize that the Lutherans were talking about much more than a blessing uttered over turkey and cranberry sauce.

Frankly, the whole "faith through grace alone" concept terrified me. I was much more comfortable "earning" my salvation, methodically checking off items on my to-do-for-God list and inching my way through the decades toward eternal life. Mail cheerful cards to Grandma Hilma in the nursing home. Check. Bake lasagna and brownies for the mom with the new baby. Check. Serve soup to the homeless at the local shelter. Check. Forgo chocolate during Lent. Check. Of course this felt right to me—everything was in *my* control. It was *my* list and *my* good deeds; I got to decide what to do and how to do it. Plus it felt good. Who doesn't get a warm, fuzzy feeling after accomplishing a dreaded but obligatory task, like visiting an aged relative in a nursing home?

While faith through grace alone is probably liberating for most people, freeing them from the inescapable burden of sin, it scared the heck out of me because it required that I relinquish control. It carried me full circle back to the aspects of God I couldn't define, hem in, deconstruct, or rationalize. It carried me back to the heart, which was a much more difficult realm to navigate than the head. Honestly, I would much rather have earned my entrance to heaven than take a flying leap onto the slippery slope of faith. Earning seemed much more predictable, orderly, and measurable, so much less fraught with fear, than leaping. Leaping into faith made me uneasy. Leaping into faith required me to trust and surrender to someone I couldn't see.

The first time I read the parable of the vineyard workers in Matthew 20, I was completely and utterly baffled. In the story, a landowner hires a group of workers in the early morning to labor for a denarius in his vineyard all day. Later in the morning, the landowner hires another group of workers, and then he does this three more times during the day: at noon, 3 p.m., and 5 p.m. When evening comes the landowner instructs his supervisor to pay all the workers their denarius, beginning with the group that was hired in the late afternoon and ending with the group hired in the early morning. Not surprisingly, the workers who toiled in the vineyard for twelve hours are furious, bitter, and resentful that their pay equals that of the slackers who labored only one measly hour.

I could totally understand the perspective of the bitter, exhausted workers who slaved all day in the hot sun for the same lousy pay as the laggards who sauntered in for a single hour of work. *What a travesty!* I thought the first time I heard this parable in church. *What a complete ripoff!* I could not fathom why in the world a boss would be so foolish as to pay the same wage for a top-notch laborer who worked tirelessly as he did for one who clearly abused the system. In my equal-pay-for-equal-work world, according to my corporate ladder ethic, this made no sense. Furthermore, I could not understand the landowner's response to one of the disgruntled workers.

> I am not being unfair to you, friend. Didn't you agree to work
> for a denarius? Take your pay and go. I want to give the one
> who was hired last the same as I gave you. Don't I have the
> right to do what I want with my own money? Or are you
> envious because I am generous? (Matthew 20:13–15)

All I could think when I heard this response was, *This is not generosity. This is sheer stupidity!*

About the third or fourth time I heard this story, I finally realized the parable wasn't about sheer stupidity, but about grace. Jesus's story did not make a bit of fiscal sense—and that was whole point. Grace does not make sense. It's not supposed to make sense. Grace cannot be calculated or formulated, earned or even rewarded for a job well done. Grace is a gift, not a salary. And none of us, not even the disciples themselves, even comes close to earning salvation; all of us are granted salvation as the ultimate gift.

I can't apply the "I'm entitled to" or the "I deserve" thought process to any part of my life, whether something as shallow as a material pursuit or as serious as my health or the well-being of my family, because it is all grace. It is all a gift. Life itself is grace. And when it comes to grace, the word *deserve* isn't even part of the equation.

———

As has been the case with many aspects of my spiritual journey, my kids have taught me more about our deep need for grace than any book or sermon. It never ceases to amaze me that no matter how much I give my children, they always want more. Enough is never enough. Like most kids, mine have moments, many moments in fact, in which they are ungrateful.

In Noah's case the primary issue is time, specifically time spent with me. No matter how much time I spend with Noah, he always wants more. I could dedicate my entire weekend to him, a full forty-eight hours of bike riding and reading and talking about Mario Bros. and Minecraft, and on Sunday night he will inevitably complain, incredulous, "What! That's it? But I didn't get enough time with you!"

This issue of time-greed was most apparent when Noah started kindergarten. He didn't want to go to school, not one bit. While his classmates danced around the sidewalk waiting for the morning bell to ring, Noah leaned heavily against my leg, his scrawny arm encircling my thigh, his big brown eyes welling. Noah was not interested in school; he preferred to stay home with me, despite the fact that I tried every reasonable tactic to convince him to embrace school and be grateful for it.

There was the rational approach: "Honey, every six-year-old goes to school. You're a big kid now, so you go to school."

The social approach: "But isn't it so much fun being with your friends all day?"

The culinary approach: "But you get to eat a yummy lunch in the cafeteria!"

The love approach: "I know, honey, I miss you too."

The tough love approach: "Listen, this is the way it is. You will go to school from now until you are at least eighteen years old...or, if you're like your father, thirty-five years old."

The bribery approach: "How about we go out for ice cream after I pick you up today?"

And finally, the guilt approach: "Honey, school is a blessing, a gift. There are many, many children in this world who never have the opportunity to go to school."

Noah was intrigued by this information. "So what do the kids do all day?" he asked.

I knew exactly where Noah was headed with this question, and I knew I would have to answer carefully to ensure this option did not sound too appealing. "Well, in some cases kids have to work, like out in the fields harvesting vegetables or in factories making clothes," I told him, figuring manual labor and sweatshop work wouldn't seem like much fun.

But this is where I underestimated Noah. "And where are their mommies?" he asked. "Where are the mommies when the kids are working in the factories?"

I struggled to stay one step ahead of Noah's thought process, but I knew right where he was going with this question. "Oh, the mommies are working in different factories, different fields, totally separate from their kids," I said, glancing at him in the rearview mirror as we drove to his school. "Yeah, absolutely, the kids work in different factories, and in fields far away, miles and miles away, kid factories and kid fields. Sometimes they don't see their mommies for like twelve or fourteen hours. Sometimes they only see their mommies on the weekends."

Noah wasn't buying it. I could tell by the look on his face, the way he bit his lip as he gazed out the window. And I was at my wit's end. The conversation had spiraled into absurdity with me literally making up material as I went along. I had succumbed to complete fabrication in order to convince my son that he should attend school happily. Finally, exasperated, I said to Noah, "Listen, honey, you just go to school. That's all there is to it. I really don't want to talk about this anymore."

And that ended the conversation. Until the next morning, when it began anew.

This went on for weeks. I woke up every morning with a pit in my stomach, dreading the conversation that would begin the minute Noah emerged from his bedroom, groggy in his gecko pajamas, tufts of hair springing like cockatoo feathers from the top of his head. No matter what I said, no matter what I did, I could not get Noah to accept that school was a blessing, that he should enjoy it, be grateful for it, experience and live it with enthusiasm. He did not see it that way at all.

My negotiations with Noah gave me a glimpse of how God might feel when it comes to us thick-skulled, impossible humans. After all, God gives us everything, right? He gives us his love, his gifts, his time, his forgiveness, his own son's life—and what do we do in return? We ignore it, dismiss it, abuse it, feel entitled to it, or want more of it. We are all a bunch of ingrates, no better than small children, always wanting more, more, more—complaining about our blessings, or worse, taking them for granted, feeling that we deserve our blessings rather than acknowledging that we've been graced with them. God, I realized, must feel like a mom sometimes, rolling his eyes and harrumphing over how ungrateful, how stubbornly flawed we are. How we neglect our gifts and our talents, make the wrong decisions and hurt other people, time and time again. This, I finally realized, is why we need grace. Because we're like children, and because we need God's forgiveness, his second and third and fourth chances, again and again. God, the best of parents, will always let us try again. He will always give us another opportunity for yet another fresh start.

The trouble is that merely *trying,* even trying *really* hard, doesn't work. My CrossWalk day was the perfect example. I tried really hard the day I launched my CrossWalk initiative, and although I had the best intentions, although I tried for a full sixteen hours to demonstrate Jesus-like behavior and attitude, in the end, as I rained Cheez-Its over my son's head, I clearly failed in my attempt to glorify God and to be like Jesus.

I once read somewhere that to become more like Jesus simply by trying is like running a marathon simply by lining up at the start line and *trying* to finish. You can't do it, even by trying really, really hard. If you aim to run a marathon without training, you'll end up prone on the sidewalk, at best frustrated, spent, and defeated; at worst injured, ill, or even dead. Instead, to run a marathon properly you must organize your life around training and arm yourself with the tools that will eventually help you achieve what seems impossible.

As Paul advised, "Run in such a way as to get the prize. Everyone who competes in the games goes into strict training.... Therefore I do not run like someone running aimlessly" (1 Corinthians 9:24–26). Paul wasn't talking about physical running but rather running the long race of the Christian faith. Just as finishing a marathon requires purpose and discipline—slowly and methodically training your body to run farther and farther; eating a balance of protein, carbohydrates, and fat; hydrating properly; and preparing your mind to overcome feelings of doubt—becoming a better Christian requires similar purpose, discipline, and training. There is only one difference. While the Christian life benefits from discipline in the forms of prayer, Bible study, and worship to help us run with vigor and stamina, it also depends on grace.

I wasn't exactly comfortable with the notion of grace, and the concept of faith through grace alone still made me more than a little uneasy, but I finally understood that grace was the key. I wouldn't, couldn't, get the prize without grace.

10

Surrendering
the Fear

> If my life is surrendered to God,
> all is well. Let me not grab it back,
> as though it were in peril in His
> hand but would be safer in mine!
>
> —ELISABETH ELLIOT

I n *Mere Christianity* C. S. Lewis argued that while it's nearly impossible to hand over our whole selves to Jesus, it's easier than the alternative, which is "to remain what we call 'ourselves,' to keep personal happiness as our great aim in life, and yet at the same time be 'good.'" These two disparate pursuits do not balance, Lewis claimed, no matter how much we desire both of them. We cannot simultaneously strive for both personal happiness and God; we cannot pursue our own needs and God at the same time. The solution, Lewis stated, is to let that "other larger, stronger, quieter life come flowing in…. Standing back from all your natural fussings and frettings; coming in out of the wind."[1]

The more of the Bible and theology I read, the more difficult this Christian life seemed. According to Lewis, on top of everything else, I needed to stop fussing and fretting? I needed to stand back from my resentment of the Goddess and her name-brand clothes and platinum hair? Stand back from the judgment of Owl Spectacles? Stand back from comparison and envy? Stand back and hand over my own needs and my whole self to Jesus at the expense of my personal happiness? I didn't like the sound of that.

For one thing, as the world's most covetous person, I knew envy was going to be awfully hard to hand over. I envied everyone, from my coworkers to my friends to my closest relatives. Everyone I knew had more money, more time, better hair, fancier clothes, a bigger bathtub, and a smaller butt than I did.

Whenever new friends visited my charming Tudor house, for example, I inevitably said, "Well, it's a little small, but you know, that's okay. We live in every part of our house. No space goes unused, and I like that." This, of course, was complete baloney. I said this because it sounded good, very green and Earth friendly, and Not-So-Big-House-Movement hip. What I truly felt, though, was that I'd been ripped off.

While my friends luxuriated in master suites located fifty yards or so from their children's rooms, I could underhand toss a Beanie Baby from a reclining position on my bed and land it squarely on Noah's braided rug across the hall. While my friends' master suites included grandiose bathrooms the size of Costco, my bathroom featured a toothpaste homage to Jackson Pollock in the porcelain sink and a ream of toilet paper unrolled into a fluffy pile like a discarded petticoat at the base of the toilet. One day I walked into my bathroom—which you can probably guess by now we share with our two boys—to find an entire package of Kotex extra-long maxi pads with wings strewn about, each pad meticulously stripped of its adhesive and affixed to the tile, fixtures, toilet, sink, and floor like some kind of postmodern art installation.

My envy problem traveled hand in hand with my love of stuff. Brad, for the record, does not have this problem. This is the man who lived several of his graduate school years in a third-floor turret. Not the third floor or even the attic space, mind you, just the *turret* of a ramshackle house in downtown Willimantic, Connecticut. I, on the other hand, might as well have erected a neon sign above my head that blared: Attention! Attention! Woman Trying to Fill Void with Stuff.

I lingered a bit too long over the Pottery Barn catalog. I coveted a little too enthusiastically my neighbor's goods—the really big house with the sunken whirlpool tub and the gourmet kitchen with the gleaming stainless steel appliances and the towering floor-to-ceiling windows with the remote-controlled blinds. Even Target wooed me, starting with those must-have platform sandals in the shoe department and proceeding with alarming intensity through Accessories, Housewares, and Health & Beauty. One day I went in for a single item—a birthday gift for my friend Viviana's son—and left with a Power Ranger, a pair of pink polka-dot gardening gloves, a bag of jalapeno and cheddar kettle chips, a chaise lounge chair, a sports bra, and a tube of Garnier Fructis Melting Masque. And this was a restrained shopping trip.

My Material Girl obsession became alarmingly apparent the morning Pastor Greg launched his "stuff sermon." I squirmed in the pew as he skimmed through several relevant Bible passages, including this one:

Do not store up for yourselves treasures on earth, where moths
and vermin destroy, and where thieves break in and steal. But
store up for yourselves treasures in heaven, where moths and
vermin do not destroy, and where thieves do not break in and
steal. For where your treasure is, there your heart will be also.
(Matthew 6:19–21)

And this one in Matthew 19, in which Jesus told a rich young
man:

If you want to be perfect, go, sell your possessions and give
to the poor, and you will have treasure in heaven. Then come,
follow me.... It is easier for a camel to go through the eye of
a needle than for someone who is rich to enter the kingdom
of God. (verses 21, 24)

When I heard this, my first reaction was, *Whew—what a relief!
I'm not rich! I'm middle class!* It didn't take more than a moment,
though, before I realized nothing was further from the truth. Of
course I was rich; I was filthy, stinking rich compared to most of the
people on this planet. I was so rich, in fact, I was never going to be able
to squeeze my rich body through that teeny needle eye into eternal life,
that was for sure.

So this was a quandary. On the one hand I loved, loved, loved my
new purse, but on the other hand Jesus instructed me to give away my
possessions and focus on serving others. As C. S. Lewis reminded me,
I couldn't embrace both personal happiness and God at the same time.
I couldn't love stuff and Jesus. One had to go.

Over time, I came to realize that buying a new purse was not actually the problem. In fact, the Bible does not state that *money* is the root of all evil, but that avarice, or greed, is. The word *greed* comes from the Greek *pleonexia,* which simply means "to want more." *Pleonexia* is the motive behind the purse purchase; it was what compelled me to desire the purse in the first place. The need for more, the *wanting* more, was the real issue.

Did I think I'd finally be content with my new purse in hand? Would the void finally be filled? We all know the answer to that. Sure, I might enjoy a shopping high for a day or two; I might even flaunt the purse to my friends for their admiring approval. But a few days of bliss, a week at most, was all the satisfaction I'd reap from that purchase, from any purchase. And then I would turn my eyes to yet another prize. Worse, it was all so easy to justify. After all, these prizes were relatively small items. I hadn't taken out a second mortgage so I could wear Manolos. I wasn't driving a Hummer. But what was the difference, really? It was all relative.

I had always been a "when…then" girl. *When* I got into college, *then* I'd be happy. *When* I got married, *then* I'd be happy. *When* we bought a house, *then* I'd be happy. *When* my thighs didn't rub together, *then* I'd be happy. *When* I had a baby, *then* I'd be happy. Would it ever end? The answer, of course, was no. It would never end if I kept measuring my joy, contentment, and fulfillment on a yardstick, chipping away at each inch and foot, mechanically checking off life's milestones. It would never end as long as I continued to compare myself to everyone else. It would never end, I would never find true joy, true contentment, until I put God, not myself, first. And not just once in a while, but all the time.

———

Greed and envy often sprung unexpectedly from deep inside me, and it was not only material wealth I coveted. I remember when Brad's brother was first diagnosed with cancer. Brad drove up to Minneapolis immediately after hearing the devastating news, and I stayed in Lincoln with Noah, staggering through the day on autopilot. I stopped at Super Saver to pick up a few groceries, and as I walked across the parking lot toward my car, I watched an elderly man hobble toward the store, feet shuffling, aged body hunched over a cane. The man had to have been 109; he looked like a remnant from the Pleistocene era. *Why can't it be him?* I thought, staring at the old man. *Why does it have to be Cary, Cary who's barely forty? Cary who has a baby and a wife and a full life ahead of him?* I felt rage and grief sweep through me, overwhelmed by the injustice of it all. I stood there in the Super Saver parking lot and practically willed death on an innocent, elderly gentleman. That day my envy sunk to a new low.

The more I thought about it, the more I realized my problem with envy arose not so much from a base greed—although greed was certainly part of it—but more from the ease with which I could convince myself that I or someone I loved "deserved" something. This attitude of entitlement often stemmed from something largely irrelevant. It didn't take much—Noah talking back one time too many, a coworker's snarky comment—for me to feel I deserved a break, a little reward, a treat to help me over the hump of my day. Less frequently, a larger, deeper sense of injustice fueled my feeling of entitlement: my brother-in-law didn't deserve to be seriously ill; our family didn't deserve to have such a grave situation with which to contend. Regardless of its focus, this sense of entitlement could be traced back to that Greek word *pleonexia.*

As I dug a little deeper into the concept of *pleonexia,* I discovered a second, more detrimental implication, beyond the rough translation "greed." *Pleonexia* also implies ruthless self-seeking and arrogance. In other words, my pride, that most foundational of sins, suggested that I deserved what I desired *more* than other people, whether it was a new purse at Target or a healthy brother-in-law. Simply trying harder not to covet wasn't a viable solution if I believed other people didn't deserve the purse or their good health as much as I and my family did. It was the arrogance part of *pleonexia* that told me I had as much right, perhaps even more right, to what I desired because I worked hard, was a decent person, and therefore *deserved* a reward.

Whether I coveted something as silly as a pretty purse or as serious as a loved one's health, the issue at the heart of my envy was a simple lack of trust. Although I believed in the existence of God, I still didn't trust him. I didn't trust that he would provide for and care for my family and me. I still wrestled with control and the desire to take care of everything myself, to make sure I wouldn't be left out or overlooked. *If I don't watch out for myself and my own loved ones, who will?* I reasoned. It was one thing to believe in God; it was another thing entirely to surrender to him, to hand him everything—my fussings and frettings, my flaws, my personal happiness, and even my fears. As a fusser and a fretter, a worrier, and a triple Type A control freak, I was nervous, insecure, and deeply uneasy with the idea of surrendering to anyone, never mind a God I couldn't see. Despite the fact that C. S. Lewis said surrender was imperative, I didn't want anything to do with it.

———

One weekend, Brad, the boys, and I visited a college friend and her husband and two children, Marcus and Jacob, in Boston. Every time I saw Marcus, I couldn't help but be in awe of him. By age one he was speaking in complete, articulate sentences, using words like *escalator* and *approximately.* By age six, his vibrant watercolors resembled early Matisse, he composed original pieces on the violin, and he was an athletic maniac. Marcus was an exceedingly bright child, a Renaissance man in miniature. I knew this about him, and usually I could swallow my envy, stand back, and admire with amazement. But not this time.

On the Saturday afternoon of our visit, I was upstairs in the guest suite when Brad poked his head into the bedroom. "Want to see something really impressive?" he asked. "Check out Marcus reading." I purposefully walked through the living room and into the kitchen, and I saw it was true. At six years old, Marcus was reading a twenty-nine-page Dr. Seuss book aloud as well as I would, better than I would, in fact. He flew through each page, not stumbling, not pausing to sound out a word, the cadence and rhyme flowing naturally and easily, each word perfectly articulated. My friend sat unfazed on the couch next to him, absently flipping through an old issue of *Better Homes and Gardens.* This was clearly not an isolated incident.

I flew back upstairs. "What is *that* all about?" I whisper-seethed to Brad. "Noah doesn't read like that. How in the world can Marcus read like that already?" I didn't wait for Brad to answer. "I know what the deal is...same thing it always is," I said. "I am so sick of the privileged people getting everything, getting ahead of everyone else. That's always the way it goes, isn't it?"

Brad looked at me, horrified. "What are you talking about?" he said, bewilderment written across his face. "So Marcus is a good reader. So what? That doesn't prove anything. What's wrong with you anyway?"

I rolled my eyes and stalked out of the bedroom. Brad didn't get it. Of course it proved something; it proved *everything*. My friend and her husband were engineers in Boston, owned a million-dollar house, drove matching Escalade SUVs to and from the suburbs. Marcus had everything; everything he touched turned to gold. And he knew it. He had the big personality to go with his myriad talents, and he bossed Noah, quiet, unassuming Noah, all weekend. Noah, who was blissfully content to swing in the hammock, admiring the sun-dappled honey locust leaves. Noah, who loved the wind whistling through the white pines. Noah, who sat on Santa's lap the year he was four years old and asked for the reference book *Designing with Succulents*. Not a Transformer, not Star Wars action figures, not even Legos for crying out loud, but a 146-page cactus garden reference book, complete with propagation tips and a 14-page index. (Santa, by the way, responded with a quizzical, somewhat troubled stare. Clearly he hadn't the faintest idea what a succulent was…and from the look on his face, he thought Noah was requesting something vaguely pornographic.)

"Why are you so angry about this? It's just a dumb kids' book," said Brad, following me into the bathroom.

"Because…b-because…," I stammered. "Because this is where it all begins, right here, with the rich, privileged kid who catapults up life's ladder, squashing everyone in his wake. The rich get ahead and the regular people get nothing. I'm sick of it."

Brad looked at me for a few seconds and then quietly said something that made me want to punch his lights out. "This isn't about Noah at all," he said stonily, as we stood next to the toilet. "It's about you."

Of course he was right. He usually is. I hate that about Brad. This was about my jealousy, my envy over the fact that I thought my friend had unfair advantages that made her life easier than mine. I was envious of her Ann Taylor clothes, her pedicured toes, her sprawling guest suite, and her organic blueberries. Plus she was prettier, smarter, had bigger boobs, and was always so revoltingly cheerful. Furthermore, I was envious that she had a "normal" kid. Marcus did regular kid things: tossed a football with his dad in the backyard; played on the local soccer team; could identify Superman and Spider-Man. Meanwhile my son named the trees in our backyard and cordially introduced them as his friends. My son asked for *Designing with Succulents* for Christmas. And instead of Pokémon cards or Stars Wars action figures, my son owned a collection of twenty-four succulent plants, all watered, pruned, and tidily arranged on a plant stand in the sunroom.

How did he get to be so different? I wondered that night in bed. *Was it that glass of wine I had at Thanksgiving before I knew I was pregnant? Maybe the alcohol destroyed his superhero gene. Or maybe it was all that cleaning I did with bleach. Maybe the bleach zapped his future propensity for sports.* I turned preposterous theories like these around and around for a few hours before a profound revelation hit me: below the surface, below my yearning for my son to be "normal," lay something deeper: I was afraid of what I could not control.

Long after that visit to Boston I realized that I often use self-blame as a defense mechanism in the face of powerlessness. My desire for Noah to be "normal," to explain away his beauty and uniqueness as a genetic malfunction, was driven by fear of what I could not control, fear of what I was afraid might someday be used against him, fear of what I had to put into God's hands. It was the same fear that compelled me to practically wish cancer on an innocent elderly man in a grocery store parking lot: fear that my husband's brother might die and there was not a thing in the world any of us could do about it. Just as I couldn't trust that Cary was in God's hands, I struggled to trust that God would take care of my children…and me.

The more I thought about it, the more I realized C. S. Lewis's suggestion that we lay aside our fussings and frettings and come in out of the wind was the only viable alternative to a life dictated by anxiety, distraction, and fear. Lewis's advice reminded me of one of my favorite lines in the Bible, which says simply, "Be still, and know that I am God" (Psalm 46:10). Lewis acknowledged that this break, this stillness, would be brief at first, a mere few moments, because he knew how difficult it was for us humans, preoccupied and distracted as we are, to be still. And for some of us—we hyper-multitaskers, those of us who covet and complain and fume—more difficult than others. But as Lewis said, even those few moments are critical because "from those moments the new sort of life will be spreading through our system: because now we are letting Him work at the right part of us."[2]

The morning after my Marcus tantrum, my friend and I sat on her patio, sipping iced tea while the kids played in the backyard. I watched as Noah invited Jacob, who had been spurned by his older brother, into his imaginary fort. I watched as Noah leaned in close, bending his head toward his young friend as he patiently explained the differences between the trees in the yard. Jacob followed Noah's elaborate explanations intently, drinking in the rare attention of an older kid. I watched as my son focused on the younger boy, listening attentively as Jacob prattled on about the fort, touching the little boy's arm every now and then to direct his gaze to a branch or leaf.

Noah, I realized then, almost always acts with generosity and compassion. He constantly reaches out to others, to the shy kid, the kid left out of the group, the kid who doesn't quite fit in. And in that moment, with that realization, I marveled in awe and wonder at how Noah is so perfectly right just as he is, so perfectly right as God made him. In that moment, I came in out of the wind, ceased my fussing and fretting, and felt a new life, a larger, stronger, quieter life spread through me. In that moment of stillness, I allowed God to work at the right part of me.

After that incident at my friend's house I thought for a long time about why I was so unwilling to surrender, so unwilling to hand over my whole self to God and to trust him entirely. The answer I discovered was simple: I was afraid. And I'd been afraid for a long time. As a kid I'd been afraid of dying, of admitting I stole the necklace, and of being branded an outcast. Later I feared telling the truth about my unbelief because I was afraid of being labeled an outsider. And still later, after I began to believe, I was afraid of faith itself because it felt too big and amorphous. I was afraid of what I couldn't define, predict, and control. As I thought more and more about this connection between my fear and my reluctance to surrender and trust, I was reminded of an unsettling and frightening event that had taken place several years prior, long before I'd even begun this journey toward faith.

Back when we were first married, Brad and I went camping in Montana's Glacier National Park. This endeavor, you should know, was big for me. I love the outdoors—I have a garden, I like to rake, I enjoy the occasional hike—but this was taking love of nature to a whole new level. Prior to this, my longest hikes had been an arduous trek up Mount Washington in New Hampshire and a few day hikes in the Colorado Rockies, so I knew I was about to venture beyond my comfort zone. That's why, when I planned this road trip, mapping our route from Brad's parents' house in Minneapolis across North Dakota's wheat fields and through Montana's pronghorn-dotted hills to the gates of Glacier, I made sure to sprinkle our journey with nights in lodgings with actual walls. I even booked one night at a bed-and-breakfast with a hot tub. That was my compromise; I balanced hiking with hot-tubbing.

Brad, on the other hand, was prepared for the wilderness. This is a man who can wear the same sweaty, mud-caked socks for three consecutive days and not care, or even notice, how foul they are. A man who knows how to siphon moldy water through a portable pump so the end result magically resembles Evian. A man who actually enjoys dining on freeze-dried beef stroganoff. A man whose idea of a dream vacation is a five-day canoe trek through the remote Boundary Waters of northern Minnesota.

We departed Many Glacier Lodge at 7 a.m. as the sun glinted golden over Swiftcurrent Lake. Our twenty-five-pound packs were stuffed with everything we would need to survive three days and two nights in the wild: a two-man tent, sleeping bags, a tiny cooking stove, the water filter, food, and warm clothes. Twenty of the twenty-five pounds in my pack were comprised of M&M'S.

We hiked most of the morning through thick forest, our breath misting into the early morning air as we yelled, "Hey, bear! Hey there, bear," every two minutes or so, clapping and whistling our way through the woods, the pine needles soft beneath our feet. The yelling wasn't exactly Zen, but it was necessary—Glacier is teeming (well, that might be too strong a word…it felt like teeming at the time, but inhabited is probably more accurate) with grizzly bears. We'd seen a bunch that very morning lolling on the mountainside, lazily combing through huckleberry bushes for breakfast. The bears were cute when they were a half mile away but not so cute when you rounded a corner in the woods and came face to face with mama bear and baby. The racket we made was a low-tech warning signal, one that would supposedly send them scampering into the woods. I was not convinced.

Five miles or so into the trek—it was about eleven to reach the campsite—I began a low-level moaning that quickly escalated into a crescendo of complaints: my neck hurt, the pack straps were searing my flesh, my feet throbbed, I was getting a blister, a fly incessantly buzzed about my head. Could we stop for a snack? I was hot. I was cold. I was hot again. Were we almost there yet? Could I have some M&M'S? I was sick of yelling to the stupid bears. Were we almost there yet? Could I have some more M&M'S?

Still, it was hard to stay grumpy in the midst of such awesome beauty. Jagged gray peaks set against a sapphire sky rose from fields of blowing wildflowers, their sunny heads bowing in the breeze. The air was so fresh, so crisp and clean, the inside of my nose actually tingled.

I felt like Maria von Trapp—well, a slightly crabbier Maria—as I stood in an open field ringed by snow-capped mountains, the land so incredibly big.

Brad erected the tent on a lovely plateau when we finally arrived, hours later, at our back-country campsite. Far below us a glacial lake sparkled the blue-green shade of Aquafresh, and above us, enveloping us, the mountains loomed. It was the most beautiful spot I had ever seen. We lazed away the rest of the afternoon, tripping down to the lake to skip stones across the dazzling water; sunning ourselves drowsy on a warm, flat rock balanced like an altar on the shore. Over our dinner of macaroni and cheese and a Hershey's Special Dark bar, we watched the mountains glow azalea pink as the sun set, and then we snuggled into our flannel and fleece for the night.

Two hours later, about midnight or so, I awakened with a jolt. The wind had picked up, and the nylon tent flapped violently as gusts shuddered across the plateau. I panicked.

I have never enjoyed wind. Some people relish the wild reckless-ness of a good windstorm, but I have always been terrified of its brute force. It makes me feel out of control, powerless, small. So there I was, perched on a pebbly plateau as the wind ripped through the valley. Suddenly I was sweating, dizzy, and nauseous.

"Brad! Brad! I feel gross! I think I'm going to throw up!" I shook him awake—of course he was sleeping peacefully through it all. "Are we okay?! The tent! The tent! It's blowing over! I think I'm going to throw up!"

Brad assured me that we were indeed okay. The sound effects were actually worse than the reality, he said; something about the tent material and its tendency to flap loudly in even the most innocuous breeze. Still, I was sweaty, my pulse pounded in my ears, and the tent felt very cramped.

"I'm just going to step outside for a minute," I told Brad, figuring the fresh air would ease my claustrophobic panic. I crawled out onto the rock in my socks and stood up. Brad was right: the wind wasn't actually that bad. It was breezy, sure, but not the gale I had imagined inside the tent. But as I gazed up at those looming mountains, the glacial snow ripping dramatic, ghostly swaths of white across the darkness, I felt unexpectedly, absolutely terrified and so, so small. A baffling mix of agoraphobia and claustrophobia swept through me as I stood on the rock shivering in my flannel pj's, my arms wrapped around my chest. The land was so monstrously vast I felt squashed, as if the mountains were an enormous vise squeezing the breath from my body. I was horrified by the reality that I was trapped—stuck in this big, lonely, scary place, eleven miles on foot from civilization in moonless, bear-ridden blackness.

I ducked back into the tent. "It's not helping!" I gasped to Brad. "I feel weird! I want to leave! Can we leave now?"

Brad stared at me in disbelief. "Now? Are you kidding? You're kidding, right?" he asked. "In the middle of the night? How exactly do you think we're going to find our way back to the lodge in the middle of the night?" I realized, of course, that he was right; leaving was impossible. I felt gaggy. I started to cry.

The rest of the night I dozed with my face pressed into a tiny opening in the zipped tent flap, trying to negotiate a balance somewhere between half in and half out of the tent. Brad was sweet and remarkably patient, especially given the fact that no one in his entire extended family had ever acted like such a wackjob on a camping trip.

At 5 a.m. we packed up our campsite and began the eleven-mile hike
back out. The next night we spent in a lodge. All in all, it was not my
best moment.

That terrible night in Glacier took place long before I believed in
God. I would like to think that if I'd had God in my life that night, I
would have handled that feeling of powerlessness in the face of vast,
oppressive awesomeness with a bit more courage. I'd like to think I
would have felt awe instead of pure terror. Yet more than a decade
after that Glacier trip, as I contemplated how I could possibly hand
myself and my sons wholly over to God, I wondered if that feeling of
fear and powerlessness was more present in my life than ever. After all,
I was still inclined to try to define God in a way my rational, concrete
mind could fathom and comprehend. I was still trying to compart-
mentalize God into a logical system that would guide me step by rational step. It was difficult for me, the woman who liked everything
to march along with military precision, to accept the fact that overwhelming vastness existed and that I could not harness it and control
it. I knew I deprived myself of the mystery and wonder of faith too
often because mystery and wonder were simply too overpowering, too
Glacier-mountain big. I knew trust was an essential part of faith, and
I also knew I didn't have it. I didn't know how to trust God with the
big stuff.

Frankly, I couldn't even trust God with the small stuff, a point
made crystal-clear during our kitchen renovation. Going into the
eight-week reno, I knew, at least on an intellectual level, that my house
would be in disarray. "I'm kind of looking forward to it actually," I said
to my mother on the phone. "It means I won't have to vacuum for
eight weeks. What am I going to do with all my free time?" I assumed

the experience would be liberating, that I would uncover my relaxed, go-with-the-flow side that had lain dormant for years.

And I was totally kidding myself.

As it turned out I could not, in fact, embrace occasional messiness, not one bit. Instead of accepting the chaos, reveling in the fact that I could abandon the vacuum and Windex, I grew more and more freakish in my zest for control, in my absolute quest for order. As the walls literally crumbled around me, I found myself on my hands and knees picking lint specks off the living room rug. Despite the fact that I was shaking plaster dust out of my underwear before dressing each morning, I couldn't stop myself from scrubbing the hard water mineral deposits off the bathroom faucet with a toothbrush. I was unbearable to be with, perpetually crabby for eight weeks. I moved about the house in restless anxiety, constantly in motion, unable to sit for even five minutes straight. On a positive note, I torched hundreds of additional calories and lost three pounds, the result of my incessant motion. The downside, though, was that my spouse and children were in hell.

I thought a lot about my tendency to control my environment in the weeks following the kitchen renovation. Even after the pots, Tupperware, and graham crackers had been restored to their rightful spots, I couldn't stop thinking about why I strove so vigilantly to maintain order in my home, not only during the upheaval of the renovation, but in the ordinary day-to-day as well. Sure I'm the daughter of a drill sergeant. Sure I love order and efficiency, but still, it seemed I took my inherent Type A tendencies to the extreme. It was clear I feared powerlessness and chaos, but I also began to suspect that my obsessive need to control was a misguided attempt at self-protection and self-preservation—and at the protection and preservation of my loved ones as well.

My brother-in-law had beaten the odds and recovered from his cancer, but even years later, our family still reeled from the shock of the diagnosis. I'd witnessed Cary's battle firsthand, I'd seen how close he had come to death, and it had scared me senseless. But nothing bad could happen to my husband or my children or me if I had everything under control, right? No tragedy or disaster could befall us if I stayed on top of every last detail, right? Order in my home and in my life gave me a false sense of security. Order let me believe I didn't have to trust my precious loved ones' lives to anyone else, including God.

The problem with this strategy (besides the fact that it doesn't work, of course) is that adherence to such extreme structure and routine doesn't allow for any spontaneity, any living. Filling my life with never-ending household minutiae—dusting, folding laundry, weeding, demineralizing—left little time for anything else. And so, as I began to dig more deeply into the "fussings and frettings" that occupied much of my time, and as I began to search my heart more deeply for what might be inhibiting my willingness to trust God, I also began to release my tight-fisted grip on the routine and structure of my day. Ever so slowly, I began to let things go.

I left the mantel dusty another hour to read *The Digging-est Dog* to Rowan, three times in a row. I put down the rake to observe a praying mantis climb the clematis. I played a game called Dump and Recycle with the kids, when in actuality, I preferred something neater and quieter like coloring or reading. Little by little, I relaxed. Bit by bit I let moments and space open up in our daily lives.

It wasn't easy. The OCD devil continued to chant her relentless refrain, and my natural instinct was always to manage the moments that comprised each day rather than sink into them, experience them, and allow them to unfurl without manipulation. These were small steps, teeny-tiny baby steps. But they were important steps because in those moments when I ceased to strive, when I ceased accomplish, when I ceased to control, I experienced God more fully than ever before. I felt him in Rowan's warm weight against my side as we turned the pages of his favorite book on the couch, the late afternoon light pooling on the hardwood floor. I saw him in the delicate, spindly limbs of the praying mantis, camouflaged perfectly amid the foliage. I heard him in the raucous laughter of my children, and in my laughter, too, as they dumped pile after pile of blocks, scattering them across the entire sunroom floor. I suspect God had been there all along as I spiffed and polished and shined my house in a flurry of motion, but I'd always been too busy to notice.

It was the kind of day in early spring that made you hold your breath in anticipation, a day just warm enough to entice with the barely plausible thought of ice cream. The kids and I sat outside Dairy Queen under the crab apple tree, contentedly licking our soft-serve cones as fragile blossoms dropped like snowflakes onto the asphalt. The air was rich with the scent of recent rain and new green, the concrete bench still so cool it seeped a wintry chill through the seat of my jeans.

Noah had finished his cone in record time and was leaping from one bench to another, while Rowan dripped rivulets of chocolate down his arm and into the crease of his elbow. I had just turned toward him with a paper napkin when Rowan burst out laughing and pointed, rainbow sprinkles falling like confetti from his fingers. When I looked at where he was pointing, I saw Noah standing atop a bench with his jeans and Bob the Builder briefs wrenched down to his knees. He was waggling his penis in the direction of a minivan parked at the drive-through, one arm arched above his head like a rodeo porn star. The husband in the driver's seat was clueless, busy balancing a carton of Blizzards, but his wife was aghast, slack-jawed as she stared at my son.

"Noah! What are you doing?!" I screeched. "Pull up your pants right now before a cop drives by and arrests you for indecent exposure!" He froze for a split second, eyes wide, before yanking his pants up. While Rowan thought the scene was hilarious, I did not see much humor in it. I have never coped well with public embarrassment and am definitely not one to handle a spectacle with grace. The frivolous novelty of ice cream on a warm spring day was ruined, and two out of the three of us sulked during the walk back home.

We didn't rehash the incident. I figured my dramatic reaction had been sufficient to convince Noah that public penis-waggling was inappropriate. A month later, though, as I hunched over the keyboard in our basement office one night, Noah appeared, standing behind me in his dinosaur pj's.

"Am I going to jail?" he blurted, his eyes filling with tears. "Am I going to jail because of Dairy Queen?"

"What in the world are you talking about?" I asked, faintly irritated that it was after nine o'clock—well into the Mommy Hours—and he was still awake and conversing with me. Turned out, of course, he was referring to, as he put it, "When I was nudie at Dairy Queen." He had mulled over the incident and my rash words each night for a full twenty-eight days before finally garnering the courage to voice his fears.

I explained that I had overstated the punishment—overreaction, Brad once wryly noted, is my modus operandi. I told Noah that the police would not, in fact, arrest him for pulling down his pants in the parking lot of Dairy Queen. I apologized more than once, mentioned it was still completely inappropriate to flash your penis at a minivan parked at the Dairy Queen drive-through, and hugged him. Noah visibly relaxed, his warm little body limp under my embrace, the strain of his impending jail sentence lifted.

After he had gone back to bed, I couldn't stop thinking about it. I felt horrible and irresponsible for terrifying him. What kind of mother was I, anyway? Wasn't I supposed to protect my child from the evils of the world, to nurture his fragile psyche rather than single-handedly destroy it? Shivering in the chilly basement that night, I felt overwhelmed, inadequate, and vastly unqualified in my role as a parent. Here was this little person, this unshaped, innocent, blooming life in *my* hands, my incompetent, destructive hands. It was all too much— too big, too important, too awesome.

In a way, I realized, Noah's fragility mirrored my own. His fear and powerlessness illustrated how terribly equipped we all are to face on our own whatever the big, mean, scary world tosses our way. And just as Noah turned to me in a moment of desperate hopelessness, I knew that I could and would have to turn to God. Noah had tried to conquer his fear by himself, lying in bed sifting through his terror each night for a month. But in the end he couldn't do it; he had to unburden himself in the face of what to him was an insurmountable problem. Likewise, in a strange twist of events, I learned that night that I needed to do the same. When life's suffering crushed me like a craggy mountain, when the world threatened to paralyze me with hopelessness and fear—fear of death, fear of illness and tragedy, fear that doubt and unbelief would resurface, fear that I couldn't keep my children safe and secure forever—I needed to turn to God and put my trust in him.

Sitting in the dark, cold basement, I stepped back from my "fussings and frettings" and turned the whole ugly mess over to God. Limp with relief, I realized I didn't need to face my faults and fears, my inadequacies and my powerlessness on my own. I have God. A God who loves me in spite of my blurting and blundering, in spite of my overreactions and foot-in-the-mouth moments. A God who forgives even my worst parenting decisions, who eases even my worst fears. I have a God who guides me over the most formidable peaks and into the most tranquil valleys.

I knew, even in the midst of that unburdening, that surrender and trust wouldn't ever be easy for me. My very nature battles it. I understood that I would have to repeat this process of surrender and trust again and again, possibly throughout my entire lifetime. But I also understood that I had a choice. The choice to trust was all mine.

11

Beloved Misfit

> We're the Messiah's misfits. You
> might be sure of yourselves,
> but we live in the midst of
> frailties and uncertainties.
> —1 CORINTHIANS 4:10, MSG

Two years after I began to ask "Why not?" I attended my friend Viviana's baptism. A handful of her close friends along with her husband, Pablo, and her three kids stood in the alcove connected to the church sanctuary. The minister performed the sacrament, dripping water from his cupped hand gently over Viviana's head and making the sign of the cross on her forehead as her husband and children encircled her. In that moment I glimpsed the profound meaning of baptism—to be cleansed, freed, and marked as a child of God. It was surprisingly emotional, and more than a few of us teared up as we stood in a circle around Viviana and her family. As I watched the brief ceremony I felt a surge of warmth and connection, not only with the people in the room, but with God.

I sort of missed out on my own children's baptisms. Back then I was still in the "going through the motions" stage of spirituality, at best ambivalent, at worst unbelieving. After Noah was born, my mom asked every few weeks, "So…did you set a date for the christening yet?" She tried to act nonchalant and conversational, but her voice was tinged with anxiety. She was fretting, and I knew why. She worried that if something tragic happened, Noah would end up bouncing around in Limbo, dependent on the prayers of strangers in order to reach heaven.

Truthfully, I didn't care much about baptizing my kids. I did it out of custom and obligation, because that's what was expected and because it was a good excuse to get the extended family together. And then there was also the baptismal gown. Worn by three generations of Brad's family and hand sewn by his great-grandmother, it was an heirloom: cascading to the floor, ivory faded to the palest yellow, delicate lace at the hem and sleeves. My mother-in-law actually had to slit the lace cuffs so we could slide Noah's pudgy wrists in—apparently infants were a bit slimmer in Grandpa Arnold's day. The beautiful gown attracted the attention of some of the older church ladies, and I glowed with satisfaction, pleased with all their fawning. That's what baptism was all about for me: an heirloom gown, my family in town, and a decent prime rib dinner afterward.

There's something to be said for being baptized as an adult, for consciously *choosing* to celebrate your relationship with God and your freedom from sin. And it felt like I did exactly that the day Viviana was baptized. Despite the fact that not a single drop of water touched my head, part of me felt as if I were baptized that day too. When I look at photographs from that morning I see Viv in her floral dress, her eyes bright and shining. And I notice I'm smiling as well, as I stand beside my friend—happy for Viviana, blessed to be there, grateful that I have been symbolically baptized along with her.

As much as I appreciate that kind of spontaneous connection with God, I've found that such moments of unmarred certainty are relatively rare, even as I have become more committed to a life of faith. "If I am a field that contains nothing but grass-seed, I cannot produce wheat," C. S. Lewis wrote in *Mere Christianity*. "If I want to produce wheat, the change must go deeper than the surface. I must be ploughed up and re-sown."[1] I still have to work at it all. I equip myself with an arsenal of tools, a spiritual formula, so to speak—Bible study, church, prayer, and community—and these tools facilitate my plowing and resowing. These are the tools that prepare my soil; these are the tools that nurture the seeds of wheat. These are the tools that help me overcome my unbelief, one long, fecund furrow at a time. The formula works. Sure, it's a crutch, even a bit regimented, but it keeps me on the path.

At the same time I always have to be wary of the formula, careful not to substitute the process of believing for actual belief itself. It's easy to become mired in theory, interpretation, and analysis, to lose the big picture in the details. It's tempting to get lost in the study, to turn to books and study groups and classes, to know all *about* God but not know God himself, to read *about* the Bible rather than read the Bible itself.

That would be like reading the driver's education manual cover to cover but never getting behind the wheel of a car. I could easily fool

myself into thinking I am genuinely living a faithful life, only to realize that while I am great at studying it, I am not actually living it. And
that's the challenge, of course. I need to remind myself constantly of
the *why* behind it all. Why am I reading the Bible? Why am I sitting
in church? Why am I studying the Bible with a group of acquain-
tances on a Friday night? Not to learn about God from a distance, as
if he were Napoleon or Alexander the Great, but to learn how to seek
God every day, in ordinary life, and to learn how to shape my life to
reflect him.

For a long time I frequently asked myself a reality-check question:
Was I living faith, or was I managing it? This was a particularly tricky
question because I often *felt* like I was living it. After all, it's pretty easy
to justify Bible study, church, and nurturing a faith community as living a faithful life. But those pieces, though important, are still only the
mechanics of faith. If I funnel all my time and energy into the mechanics, I feel very busy and very important and very "good," but in
the end I am still nothing more than a spiritually vapid shell. I suspected God really didn't want me to think about faith or study faith;
he simply wanted me to be faith-full—to sink into faith, to let my life
be absorbed by it and saturated with it. I could read all about faith, talk
about it, dissect it, and yearn for it, but eventually I had to take the
leap—into belief, into him—with an open heart and arms spread
wide, trusting that he will catch me and carry me.

For me, that leap of faith means asking "Why not?" again and
again and again. I consciously choose to take that leap, to ask that
definitive question every day. Faith is a decision I make day in and day
out, without all the proper information at my disposal and without all
the evidence neatly arranged. Faith is, as Hebrews 11:1 says, being sure

of what I hope for and certain of what I cannot see. And the fact that I am given the chance to make the decision every day is, I understand, an opportunity made possible by God's grace. God gave me free will to make that choice, and through his grace he made it possible. The further I walk on the journey, the more I know this to be true.

Can I just say, though, that unbelief was a heck of a lot easier? To not believe, to stagnate as I did for decades, was a cinch. For starters, unbelief was a habit; it allowed me to be lazy. It required nothing of me, and the longer I lived there, the deeper its roots reached. In the language of addiction psychology, I enabled my own unbelief.

It all worked out rather neatly for a while. But as Kathleen Norris wrote in *Amazing Grace,*

> In order to have an adult faith, most of us have to outgrow and unlearn much of what we were taught about religion. Growing up doesn't necessarily mean rejecting the religion of our ancestors, but it does entail sorting out the good from the bad in order to reclaim what has remained viable....
>
> The temptation to simply reject what we can't handle is always there; but it means becoming stuck in a perpetual adolescence, a perpetual seeking for something, *anything,* that doesn't lead us back to where we came from.[2]

For nearly two decades I simply rejected what I couldn't handle— not only the frightening idea of eternal punishment, but also the overwhelming thought of a vast, awesome, all-powerful, and all-knowing God—because I thought it was easier. While it was true that some aspects of Catholicism didn't work for me, here's where I made a grave mistake: In rejecting religion in its entirety, I rejected God too. In dismissing my religion, I dismissed the possibility of belief altogether.

And then I began the perpetual seeking, as Norris observed, for something, anything—anything except religion and God—to fill its place. I assumed seeking God would naturally lead me right back to where I began. And that, it turned out, was a flawed assumption indeed. In fact, yanking my head out of the sand to begin sorting and reclaiming, to begin seeking, was far less frightening than wholesale rejection. The longer the fear of unbelief simmered in my subconscious, the bigger it became. Admitting unbelief was, ironically, the first step toward unburdening myself of that fear and the first step toward reclaiming faith.

In his book *The Case for Faith*, Lee Strobel noted that sincerity and truthfulness often open the door toward salvation. Strobel quoted Christian theologian Ravi Zacharias, who told him, "Sincerity is not salvation. But I think sincerity brings about the possibility of God revealing himself to you."[3] My quest for faith began with sincerity—with admitting to myself that I did not believe in God. After all, I never would have been open to the possibility of God if I hadn't first admitted to myself that I had doubts. Declaring my unbelief was the first step; declaring my unbelief allowed me to begin to seek authentically. If I hadn't faced this truth head-on, I would have persisted in my pretend faith, perpetuating the false notion that I believed while in reality practicing faith in name only.

It was my place, my relocation to Nebraska, that allowed me to experience the truth of my unbelief so bluntly. I often wonder whether I ever would have faced that truth if I had remained comfortably wrapped in the status quo, embraced by the family, friends, home, familiar surroundings, and reassuring traditions of my life in Massachusetts. After all, it was only when I was stripped of my armor, left vulnerable and exposed, alone with my wailing infant and my unfamiliar, barren life in Nebraska, that I finally faced the questions that had lurked below the surface for decades. Only when I faced the fact that I didn't belong, didn't fit in, and had lost myself entirely did I begin to ask questions and search for truth.

"[God] marked out their appointed times in history and the boundaries of their lands," Paul preached to the Athenians. "God did this so that they would seek him and perhaps reach out for him and find him, though he is not far from any one of us" (Acts 17:26–27). The very first time I read Paul's words they rang true. I had found my right place, my exact place, my one true home—not in an earthly place but in God. God had placed me in Nebraska so that I would seek, reach out for, and find him.

Strobel suggested that sincerity and truthfulness segue to salvation; my experience corroborated that theory. Although circumstances were the catalyst behind my return to church, far more than mere circumstance ignited the process. Truthfulness had exposed a chasm of despair and allowed me to feel vulnerable and afraid, perhaps for the first time in my life. The hard fact of my faithlessness opened a void within me, a space for God to slide in. Attending church wedged that crack open wider. In the beginning I floundered badly. I thought *perhaps* I desired faith, but I was positively bewildered as to how to "achieve" it. So I went to church, mostly because I didn't know how else to find faith.

Lutheranism's familiarity appealed to me. Many of the prayers were similar or even identical to those I had recited as a Catholic, and even the service unfolded in the same format. I fell into the rhythm of church without too much apprehension, going through the motions as I had done decades prior. But the surprising message of love and grace snuck up on me. It caught me off-guard, stealthily creeping into my mind and soul before I was even cognizant of it. Slowly I opened my ears and listened; tentatively I opened my heart and let the message seep in. And that's how I realized, bit by bit, that this God of love and grace couldn't have been more different than the deity I'd thought I understood as a child. The familiarity of the liturgy enticed me in the beginning, but it was the radical embrace of grace and love, the embrace of Jesus, really, that inspired me to stay.

Two years ago on Easter Sunday afternoon I opened my in-box to discover an e-mail from Kim, the girl from whom I'd stolen the necklace thirty-five years earlier, way back in the third grade. She'd come across my blog, read the story I'd written about the stolen necklace— *her* necklace—and had e-mailed to tell me that she was, in fact, the girl.

The tone of her e-mail was less than pleased, as you can imagine. I read her brief note three times, my stomach churning more with each word. And as I read, I realized I had never once considered her story in the three decades that had passed. So wrapped up in my own guilt and spiritual angst, I never once considered how she must have felt the day she realized her necklace was gone, stolen by a classmate right out of her own desk. I never once imagined how she'd undoubtedly felt betrayed, targeted, isolated, and scorned. And I never considered how she might feel should she read about the incident thirty-five years later—how it might open old wounds, tear open scars never entirely healed.

I agonized for a few hours before I finally replied to her e-mail and apologized not only for stealing her necklace but also for wounding her. My classmate graciously accepted my apology, insisting that it was a long time ago and apologies were not necessary. We exchanged several e-mails, each of us sharing a little bit of our story, a little bit of the old hurt and shame that had unexpectedly risen to the surface. And when Kim concluded her last e-mail with this statement—"I wish you peace, love, and happiness for the rest of your life"—I felt gratitude, joy, and relief. The truth had set me free. And I sincerely hope it freed her too.

Clearly no story is too small for God. As well as I thought I understood the depth of God's love and compassion, I was astounded by the fact that he cared enough to bring two women together in love and forgiveness after more than thirty-five years. So often I forget that God's plan is much bigger than any I can ever envision. I forget that he always works to bring everything together for good, no matter how small the story, no matter how bad, ugly, or broken it all looks at the start. I was prepared to receive my former classmate's ire, to suffer the consequences of my wrongdoing, but instead I received from her forgiveness and love.

I don't call it a coincidence that Kim stumbled upon my blog, read the story of her stolen necklace, and responded with a personal e-mail. I call it a miracle. I truly see the resolution of the stolen necklace as one in a long line of miracles along this tumultuous journey from unbelief to faith. God turned a bad choice into an unexpected and undeserved blessing, and this, I see now, is exactly what he has done every step of the way. I denied God for decades. I turned away, refused his love, refused to acknowledge his very existence. And what did he do in return? God forgave me. And like that one lost sheep in one hundred, he did not cease his pursuit of me until I was safe in his loving embrace.

My faith journey has taken a twisting, undulating path rather than a linear route—a winding New England road rather than a straight midwestern avenue. Often it felt as if nothing were happening at all, or worse, that I was tumbling off the path entirely or backtracking rather than moving forward. But as Henri Nouwen wrote,

> When I think that I am only distracted, just wasting my time, something is happening too immediate for knowing, understanding, and experiencing. Only in retrospect do I realize that something very important has taken place.... God is closer to me than I am to myself and, therefore, no subject for feelings or thoughts.[4]

When I look back, so many experiences in the last few years illustrate that change was underway, even when I couldn't see it in the moment. God was always close to me; I simply hadn't recognized him.

That morning at Viviana's baptism I saw, just for a moment, that something important had been taking place all along. I glimpsed my spiritual growth; I saw that progress had been made. As I stood behind the baptismal font, I felt the presence of the Holy Spirit with us in that

room, and I felt myself open wide to accept the invitation to experience
the fruits of the Spirit, as Paul called them: love, joy, peace, patience,
kindness, goodness, faithfulness, gentleness, and self-control. In those
flashes of illumination—in the Minneapolis airport, at Viv's baptism,
in the garden with Klee Klee and my kids—I felt God's presence, if
only for a moment. For me, there would be no road to Damascus, no
bolt of lightning, no white-light revelation. I was finally okay with
that. My intention, my choice, the choice God gave me, was to seek.
And in seeking I find, again and again.

These moments of epiphany did not mean, of course, that I would
cease to question altogether. Questioning, I came to understand and
accept, is part of who I am. Skepticism is woven into my fabric. But I
had shifted my approach. Instead of grappling with the questions,
wrestling them and trying to wrangle definitive answers out of them,
I simply began to strive, as the poet Rainer Maria Rilke advised, to live
with and in the questions. "Have patience with everything that is un-
solved in your heart and…try to cherish the questions themselves,"
wrote Rilke in *Letters to a Young Poet*.

> Do not search now for the answers which cannot be given you
> because you could not live them. It is a matter of living every-
> thing. Live the questions now. Perhaps you will then gradually,
> without noticing it, one distant day live right into the answer.[5]

I still seek, but I do not necessarily seek the hard-and-fast answer
anymore. Instead, I live the questions, trusting I will live into God's
answers. "Jesus invites everybody to jump," wrote Rob Bell in *Velvet
Elvis*. "And saying yes to the invitation doesn't mean we have to have it

all figured out."[6] In fact, I've come to realize the opposite should be true: I should *not* have it all figured out. And if I think I do, I should take that as a red flag because it probably means I have crafted a God of my own design, a God whom I can control. Living the questions and relinquishing control is so much more challenging than fashioning a God who is entirely fathomable and comprehensible. But living the questions is also more real—a truer, more honest approach to discovering and nurturing a relationship with God.

For a long time I was waiting for the perfect moment to declare my faith: the moment I had everything figured out, all the questions answered, the wrestling match finished. In the past I assumed my faith would "begin" when all my questions had answers, when I felt a certain way, when I acted in a certain way. I was waiting for all the pieces to fall into place so I could declare once and for all, without a shadow of a doubt, that I believed in God.

The reality, of course, is that the pieces of my faith had been falling into place all along. Asking "Why not?" was my way of surrendering, of accepting that *the* single, perfect moment, the moment when my questions were finally answered once and for all, was never going to happen. Asking "Why not?" was my way of realizing I could jump *and* still have questions. I didn't know it at the time, but asking "Why not?" was my way of saying yes to Jesus's invitation to jump.

————————

It's been six or seven years since I first began to ask "Why not?"—long enough that I've lost track of the exact time frame. I've come a long way since those early days of faith. I pray a lot more regularly now. I even read the Bible almost every day. I'm still a member of the same Lutheran church in Lincoln and the same small group, and I pray aloud with them from time to time (although it may never appear on my list of Favorite Things).

In spite of all that, I often still feel like a spiritual misfit in a lot of ways. A few months ago, during the Sunday morning worship service at a writing retreat in Texas, the minister asked us to participate in a meditative exercise. "I want you to close your eyes and listen as I read the story of Jesus and the miracle of the loaves and fishes," she said. She asked us to listen to the words and slowly let ourselves find our place in the story. "Imagine you are there," she instructed. "Picture yourself in the scene."

I squirmed in my chair a bit, and as the minister began to read from the Bible, I peeked (you know I did, right?) to make sure everyone else in the sanctuary had their eyes closed too. They did. So I closed my eyes and let myself be immersed in the reading. I listened to the minister's soothing voice as she read about the day Jesus turned a few loaves of bread and a couple of fish into enough food to feed a crowd of five thousand. As instructed, I tried to visualize myself as a participant in the actual event.

Later over lunch a few of us shared our thoughts on the experience. My friend Nancy told us she had seen herself right there in the middle of the crowd, passing out the bread and fish with the disciples themselves. She saw herself carrying a basket, handing out loaves. A couple of other women at my table shared similar sentiments. We all agreed it had been an insightful and fruitful exercise. "So, where were you, Michelle?" Nancy asked, her warm brown eyes meeting mine across the table. "Where were you in the story?"

I hesitated, reluctant to admit where I had seen myself. "I was on the outside," I said, laughing nervously. "I was on the very outside of the crowd, looking in, craning to get a glimpse of the action. That's where I always am. On the outside." I sighed, ashamed and disappointed. *How in the world can you possibly still be on the outside, after all this time?* I thought to myself. I felt like a faith failure once again.

Later that afternoon on the flight home I was still thinking about the loaves and fishes exercise, recalling how I had pictured myself on the edge of the crowd, peering in, an outsider. *Is that really where I am?* I thought. *Still dancing tentatively around the outer circle? Still unsure of myself in faith? Still feeling like I don't fit in, like I don't belong, after all these years?* I gazed out the window, glimpsing patchwork plains through the sunlit cumulous clouds. And then, like a shaft of sunlight piercing the darkness, I realized that my place in the crowd doesn't matter to God.

Jesus, I remembered, loved the outsiders. In fact, he gravitated especially toward the people who didn't quite fit in, the people on the edge. He was chastised by the Pharisees for hanging around with the wrong crowd: the tax collectors and the prostitutes, the sinners and the Samaritans—the people on the fringe, the people who didn't do religion or society right. Jesus chose the outcasts and loved the misfits. Jesus came to heal not the ones who had already been found but the lost, the weak, and the hopeless. He came to heal those on the outside, the ones teetering on the edge. Jesus, I remembered, came to heal me.

It didn't matter whether I was front and center, distributing the loaves and fishes with the disciples themselves, or out on the fringe, peering in, feeling a bit unsure, a bit awkward and out of place. God loved me no matter what my place, no matter what my role.

My stomach dropped as the plane began its final descent into Nebraska. I gazed out the tiny window at the luminous clouds and the quilt of farm fields spread out far below. And I knew right then in my heart and soul, in spite of all my dithering and doubting, my wrestling for control, and my despair of ever getting it right, that God loves me exactly as I am, his beloved misfit.

Acknowledgments

This book had a long gestation. As my friend Andrea observed, "It was like birthing an elephant." I say more like birthing a Tyrannosaurus rex (or rather, laying the ginormous egg). Suffice to say, in the last seven years a great number of people have helped me along the way, and for that I am profoundly grateful. I offer my deepest gratitude to:

Laura Barker, my editor at Convergent, and the entire Convergent team who shaped and guided this story from a holey, clunky manuscript to the final, polished book. You are all so very good at what you do.

Rachelle Gardner, my agent, who took a major leap of faith in signing a no-name writer and who never gave up on this memoir.

Rachel Held Evans and Kathy Richards for generously recommending my work to Rachelle Gardner. And Steve Parolini (a.k.a. the Novel Doctor) for your editing genius.

Jeanine DeRusha, Buzz and Maureen DeRusha, Anita Ducey, Brad Johnson, Jon and Janice Johnson, Vanessa and Cary Johnson, Michaella Kumke, Viviana Morales, Pastor Greg Olson, Andrea Richards, Kristin Ronan, and Kim Turnage—for generously reading early drafts of the manuscript when I foisted them on you and offering spot-on suggestions and encouragement.

My blog readers, for your encouragement and support. I started writing the blog to build a platform, and we ended up building friendships instead. I am so grateful to you for sticking with me over the long haul.

The Edgies, for being the perfect mini focus group during the title selection process. And for serving up good food, good reads, the occasional bag of hand-me-downs, and lots of laughs.

THC Prayer Warriors, for laughter, hugs, and, of course, your prayers.

Kirstin Cronn-Mills, for mentoring me in writing, publishing, and life in general from afar.

Ann Hamilton, for gently but persistently suggesting I make that appointment with Pastor Greg.

Southwood Lutheran Church—especially my pastors, Greg Olson, Michael Ryan, and Sara Spohr—for encouraging my questions, even the ones that raised eyebrows. And my small group and church community for accepting and loving me, waffly doubts and all.

Jennifer Dukes Lee, for penciling me into Tuesdays on your prayer calendar and praying for me and this book every single week.

Deidra Riggs, for always reminding me that you'd bring me water at my first book signing, long, long before I had any hope of a book signing. God knew exactly what he was doing that night he placed us in the same line for coffee at The Mill. Thank you for being my person.

Andrea Richards, BFF extraordinaire, for having the guts to tell me which parts of the early drafts of this book were boring. You are woven right into my very fabric, and I can't imagine life without you.

My late in-laws, Jon Johnson, for handing over your whole pile of

Barnes & Noble gift cards so I could buy my very first Bible, and Janice Johnson, for your quiet but powerful example of faith. You are gone from this world but never forgotten in my heart.

My sister, Jeanine, for talking me off the cliff all twenty-six times I quit writing. And for saying, "Did you think you wouldn't get any?" when I bawled after receiving the first of many rejections.

My parents, Maureen and Buzz, for your love, support, encouragement, and example of faith. And for not wigging out when I became a Lutheran. Dad, I am so glad you were the very first person to buy a copy of this book.

Noah and Rowan, for showing me God's gifts every single day. I love you both so much (even when you bring live bugs into the house).

Brad, most especially, for always having faith that I would find faith and for urging me time and time again to keep writing my story. I love you, Gray Hair, light of my life.

And finally, thank you God, for pursuing me, fighting for me, and holding on to me by the scruff of my neck. I know I'm stubborn. I'm sure glad you are too.

Notes

Chapter 1

1. *The Catholic Encyclopedia,* s.v. "scapular," www.newadvent.org/cathen/13508b.htm.

Chapter 3

1. Edward Abbey, *Desert Solitaire* (New York: Ballantine, 1971), 1.
2. Dante Alighieri, *The Divine Comedy* (New York: Vintage, 1959), 11.

Chapter 4

1. Anne Lamott, *Traveling Mercies: Some Thoughts on Faith* (New York: Anchor, 2000), 100.

Chapter 5

1. John Wesley, "Journal of John Wesley," *Christian Classics Ethereal Library,* www.ccel.org/ccel/wesley/journal.vi.ii.xvi.html.
2. C. S. Lewis, *Surprised by Joy: The Shape of My Early Life* (New York: Harcourt, 1955), 224.
3. Donald McCullough, *If Grace Is So Amazing, Why Don't We Like It?* (San Francisco: Jossey-Bass, 2005), 105–6.

4. Thomas Merton, *Conjectures of a Guilty Bystander* (Garden City, NY: Doubleday, 1966), 141.

Chapter 6

1. Barbara Owen, ed., *Steadfast in Your Word: Daily Reflections from Martin Luther* (Minneapolis: Augsburg Fortress, 2002), 78.
2. C. S. Lewis, *Mere Christianity* (New York: Macmillan, 1960), 136.

Chapter 7

1. Kathleen Norris, *Amazing Grace: A Vocabulary of Faith* (New York: Riverhead, 1998), 42.
2. Dr. Charles Bethea, quoted in Benedict Carey, "Long-Awaited Medical Study Questions the Power of Prayer," *The New York Times,* March 31, 2006, www.nytimes.com/2006/03/31 /health/31pray.html?pagewanted=all&_r=0.
3. Bob Barth, quoted in Carey, "Long-Awaited Medical Study Questions the Power of Prayer."
4. Donald Miller, *Blue Like Jazz: Nonreligious Thoughts on Christian Spirituality* (Nashville: Thomas Nelson, 2003), 239.
5. "The Hubble Ultra Deep Field in 3D," Deep Astronomy with Tony Darnell, http://hubblesite.org/explore_astronomy/deep _astronomy/episodes/4 and "Hubble's Deepest View of the Universe Unveils Bewildering Galaxies across Billions of Years," http://hubblesite.org/newscenter/archive/releases/1996 /01/text/.

Chapter 8

1. Norris, *Amazing Grace,* 66.
2. Thomas Merton, *Life and Holiness* (New York: Herder and Herder, 1963), 5.

Chapter 9

1. Norris, *Amazing Grace,* 296.
2. Lewis, *Mere Christianity,* 162.

Chapter 10

1. Lewis, *Mere Christianity,* 168–69.
2. Lewis, *Mere Christianity,* 169.

Chapter 11

1. Lewis, *Mere Christianity,* 168.
2. Norris, *Amazing Grace,* 24–25.
3. Ravi Zacharias, quoted in Lee Strobel, *The Case for Faith: A Journalist Investigates the Toughest Objections to Christianity* (Grand Rapids, MI: Zondervan, 2000), 162.
4. Henri J. M. Nouwen, *The Genesee Diary: Report from a Trappist Monastery* (New York: Doubleday, 1976), 120.
5. Rainer Maria Rilke, *Letters to a Young Poet* (Mineola, NY: Dover Publications, 2002), 21.
6. Rob Bell, *Velvet Elvis: Repainting the Christian Faith* (Grand Rapids, MI: Zondervan, 2005), 28.